When God Disappoints: Character Studies in the Bible

A supplement to When God Disappoints: Lessons from Jonah

Ken Hathcoat

1

ISBN: 1482709937
ISBN-13: 978-1482709933

CONTENTS

CONTENTS

THE IMPORTANCE OF EXAMPLE

There was a reason I chose Jonah as the main character of study for my book, *When God Disappoints.* Jonah is like most Christian men and women I know. He knew God and loved Him. He showed courage and endurance in the journey God had given him. He was generally honest with himself and with God, but he also got mad at God and was frustrated with the direction of his life. Specifically, he was frustrated with what he saw as inconsistencies in what God said about Himself versus how God acted in his personal world.

I can identify with the very imperfect Jonah much more so than other prophets in the Old Testament. Those other prophets sometimes seem more obedient and committed to God, opposed to an ordinary, dirty rotten sinner like me. Jonah is the Old Testament version of Peter. If there was an

5

opportunity to stick his foot in his mouth or clumsily stub his toe on something, Peter would be the one to do it. Peter was the one who would brashly claim to never deny Christ, only to do so three times a few hours later (Matthew 26:30-35; 69-75).

Peter was also the only mortal man in history to walk on water. He, along with John and James, were the only ones to see Christ transfigured with Moses and Elijah. And Peter was chosen—by Christ Himself—as the leader of the apostles. God accomplished a lot through this very ordinary, unremarkable man, just like He did through Jonah. To me, Jonah is the perfect example of a sinful, disappointed man whom God used greatly in spite of himself. Like Peter, he offers hope to any man or woman wrestling with disappointment in God.

In the middle of teaching a class on disappointment in God—using the Bible studies found at the end of the first five chapters of *When God Disappoints*—I realized two things. One was that while I had given several biblical characters to study regarding specific aspects of being disappointed in God, it became clear to me that I had not given enough *direction* in examining those individuals. I generally don't like fill-in-the-blank Bible studies, so I wanted readers to come to their own conclusions about what they thought was happening regarding disappointment with God in these people's lives.

However, I'm not sure what I wanted to happen was occurring. It was like an art teacher taking his students to a mural-size painting of a landscape and then simply asking them what they saw. The class could answer the question with terse brevity ("Clouds, grass, hills, trees") or they could write a seven page essay. Both answers would be correct, but the first answer would likely not have been what the teacher intended. Like the art teacher in my example, I hoped those in my class would get much more out of those biblical examples.

The second thing I realized is that *the lessons* I wanted those Scriptures to impart were not easily being noticed, which was not the fault of the studier. It was *my* fault. I wasn't clever enough to lead them to those lessons, so the only way I knew how to make that happen was to directly point out the applications.

That is the point of this book. I want to examine the biblical lives of eighteen men and women who wrestled with issues related to being disappointed in God and show how their struggles parallel our own disappointments.

There is a lot we can learn from examples in the Bible. Jesus emphasized parables in His teachings, and many of the stories in the Bible are given as real-life instruction on how we should live. Not just in the "what to do/what not to do," but in the revealing of how and why God acts over the course of our life and the consequences of those choices long after our life is over. In these biblical examples, we have the advantage of viewing each life from 30,000 feet. We typically see the beginning, middle and end of their lives, as well as the long-range outcomes of the decisions they made in their lives.

We won't be discussing the first Bible study from *When God Disappoints* regarding God's character. Not because it's unimportant. On the contrary, it's more critical than any of the other four studies combined. However, in the space of this book, it would be difficult to do justice to the study of God's character and attributes regarding being disappointed in God. As I mentioned in the first chapter, it is enough to stay focused on the fact that it is impossible for God to do evil or to lie. That means He is perfectly loving and sinless in everything He does (or allows), and that anything He has ever said is always true. If those facts are imbedded in a person's heart, the truth of those facts alone will carry any man or woman through the darkest disappointment in God.

1 Corinthians 10:11
"Now these things happened to them as an example, **but they were written down for our instruction,** *on whom the end of the ages has come."*

The purpose of this book is to examine the lives of men and women who dealt with disappointments and struggles. It is my hope that in comparing their similar struggles with ours, we can learn about God, ourselves, and our own disappointments with God.

We'll begin with the storms of disappointment.

DISAPPOINTMENT IN THE STORM

I mentioned in chapter two of *When God Disappoints* that God brings storms into our lives for a variety of reasons. But when I examine Scripture, I see there are chiefly four reasons storms can arise:

Rebuke

Amos 4:6-11

*"I gave you cleanness of teeth in all your cities, and lack of bread in all your places, **yet you did not return to me**," declares the LORD.[7] "I also withheld the rain from you when there were yet three months to the harvest; I would send rain on one city, and send no rain on another city; one field would have rain, and the field on which it did not rain would wither; [8] so two or three cities would wander to another city to drink water, and would*

not be satisfied; **yet you did not return to me,"** declares the LORD.

[9] *"I struck you with blight and mildew; your many gardens and your vineyards, your fig trees and your olive trees the locust devoured;* **yet you did not return to me***," declares the LORD.*

[10] *"I sent among you a pestilence after the manner of Egypt; I killed your young men with the sword, and carried away your horses, and I made the stench of your camp go up into your nostrils;* **yet you did not return to me***," declares the LORD.* [11] *"I overthrew some of you, as when God overthrew Sodom and Gomorrah, and you were as a brand plucked out of the burning;* **yet you did not return to me***," declares the LORD.*

Storms can come into our lives as a rebuke from God. Repeatedly in the Old Testament, God sent prophets to warn and rebuke His people when they were not following Him. When that did not work—when they refused to listen to His Word and repent—He sent His rebuke through *troubling circumstances.* Obviously, any time trouble arises, it doesn't mean God is trying to get our attention on some evil that we haven't dealt with in our lives. (That was the point Job's friends missed regarding Job's calamity.) But it is more than fair to ask ourselves when circumstances in our lives are "going south," is there something wrong in our lives in which God is trying to get our attention and wants us to change?

Refinement

1 Peter 4:12

*"Beloved, do not be surprised at the fiery trial when it comes upon you **to test you**, as though something strange were happening to you."*

Proverbs 17:3

*"The crucible is for silver, and the furnace is for gold, **and the LORD tests hearts**."*

I appreciate Wuest's translation of 1 Peter 4:12:

*"Divinely loved ones..., stop thinking that the **smelting process** which is [operating] among you and which has come to you for the purpose of testing [you], is a thing alien to you..."*

When God tests His people, it can be to show us whether we are as mature or as committed as we think we are, as Jesus did with Peter during the Last Supper or as God did when He asked Abraham to offer Isaac as a sacrifice. It could be to change some attitude or behavior that we were not aware of so that we will be more Christlike, as God did with Paul and his companions (2 Corinthians 1:8-9). Regardless of the exact reason, the purpose of the storm He sends is for purifying. In much the same way the furnace burns off impurities and leaves the slag in the processing of gold or silver, God sends storms to sanctify us. The purpose is not to destroy (as Satan's purpose was with Job). The purpose is to make us more like Him.

Suffering as He Suffered
2 Timothy 3:12
"*Indeed, all who desire to live a godly life in Christ Jesus **will be persecuted**...*"

John 15:20
"*Remember the word that I said to you: 'A servant is not greater than his master.' **If they persecuted me, they will also persecute you.** If they kept my word, they will also keep yours.*"

It is not a popular topic for most Christians, but it is true, nevertheless: as Christians, we have been called to suffer. What makes this topic more difficult is there is not always an obvious "why" in the suffering. There may not be a rebuke that needs to happen in our life. There may not be any clear lessons that we see we are supposed to be learning. There are at least two things we can conclude from the Bible about suffering:

1) *Suffering produces character* (Romans 5:3), but the visible results of suffering may not be apparent in this life. Those acts of suffering we have patiently endured may only show their fruit in the eternal future.

2) Part of our Christian life is *sharing and enduring suffering as Jesus did,* that we may gloriously reign with Him (2 Timothy 2:11-12). Of course, that doesn't necessarily mean things like scourging, beatings, and crucifixion, but things like loneliness, betrayal, and rejection by others.

Glorifying God

John 11:1-4

*Now a certain man was ill, Lazarus of Bethany, the village of Mary and her sister Martha. ² It was Mary who anointed the Lord with ointment and wiped his feet with her hair, whose brother Lazarus was ill. ³ So the sisters sent to him, saying, "Lord, he whom you love is ill." ⁴ But when Jesus heard it he said, "This illness does not lead to death. **It is for the glory of God, so that the Son of God may be glorified through it.**"*

Glorifying God can be a catch-all statement. That is, it can seemingly mean nothing, because everything ultimately glorifies God. According to

Romans 9:17, even the wicked were created to show God's goodness and mercy (that is, to glorify Him). In Sunday school, children think the right answer to just about any question is either "Jesus" or "God." So too in suffering, "the spiritually correct" answer can be, "It brings glory to God."

But there are often specific episodes in our lives where storms tangibly and measurably (in human terms) *do* glorify God. In *When God Disappoints*, I spoke of how Lazarus' resurrection not only glorified God in Mary's personal storm, but also how both Mary and Lazarus saw that his resurrection ultimately brought many people to Christ. In that event for those two people, there was a hidden "dollar bill on the ground" that neither of them could have seen at the time.

In a similar way, we may endure storms in our lives that, in both the short and long term, have God-glorifying consequences that we can't immediately see. It is only after the passage of time that we notice what God has done through those storms.

In the next four chapters, we'll examine people who went through each of these types of storms. Like many of the people in the Bible we'll look at throughout this book, one could point to several different reasons why these individuals might have had to pass through the trials they endured. But as I examine these individuals and their storms, usually one dominant theme stands out.

The first is Jacob. His is the storm of rebuke.

1 JACOB—THE STORM OF REBUKE

Genesis 25:24-26
*²⁴ When her days to give birth were completed, behold, there were twins in her womb. ²⁵ The first came out red, all his body like a hairy cloak, so they called his name Esau. ²⁶ Afterward his brother came out with his hand holding Esau's heel, **so his name was called Jacob.***

Jacob came out of his mother's womb seemingly trying to keep Esau from being the firstborn son. So they named him Jacob (*supplanter, deceiver*). Unfortunately, the name was not given based on a freak coincidence or accident. It seems his name was divinely given, for his name exemplified a trait that Jacob would contend with all his life.

You are probably familiar with the story of Jacob from Genesis 25:19 through Genesis 49. Here are the brief, bullet point facts of his life:

- Two very different boys grow up to be two very contentious young men.
- The strife is made more difficult in the home because dad (Isaac) loves the older son (Esau) but mom (Rebekah) loves the younger (Jacob).
- Rebekah helps Jacob cheat Esau out of his birthright.
- Jacob flees to distant kin and falls in love with a beautiful girl (Rachel).
- The father of that beautiful girl (Laban) tricks Jacob into marrying his older daughter (Leah). Jacob still marries Rachel, as well.
- Jacob and Esau eventually reconcile.
- Jacob fathers twelve sons through his two wives and their maids.
- Jacob's favorite son (Joseph) is despised by his brothers and sold into slavery to live in Egypt.
- After a devastating famine and the miraculous rise to power of Joseph in Egypt, Jacob and his sons journey to Egypt to live out their days.

That's essentially Jacob's story. No Hollywood writer could have composed a more imaginative plot line, and if this story were not taken from the pages of Scripture, even most Christians would have a hard time swallowing it as fact. We will return to this story five more times in this book, but for now, we need to focus on Jacob and a few key points in his life.

Jacob's character

Jacob had to have known from Rebekah that he was destined to rule over his brother. If he was her favorite, she must have told him the promise God made to her. Good news for him, but Isaac seems to care more for Esau, so how could this promise possibly be fulfilled? Here's one way: Jacob will coax Esau out of his birthright. He knows Esau is not a high-minded fellow, so he'll sell him a meal for his birthright. Esau agrees (Genesis 25:27-34), but Jacob doesn't realize that Esau's word doesn't mean much.

I realize Hebrews 12:16-17 interprets this act harshly—as it should—regarding *Esau's* disdain for the holy and honorable right of the firstborn blessing. But ask yourself this question: What kind of person would try to get his older brother to *sell* something as holy as this? It likely would not happen, but imagine a Christian man asking his older brother to *sell* his spiritual gift(s) to him. What would that behavior say about the younger brother? Esau's actions were despicable regarding his disdain for the birthright, but Jacob trying to tempt him out of his birthright resembles Satan's character much more than it does a chosen one of God.

Of course, Jacob's plan doesn't work, so Rebekah helps Jacob hatch a better plan to take the birthright. And it works! But Jacob not only swindles Esau, he deceives his father. On top of that, he allows his mother to deceive her husband. All because he felt he knew a better way to get the birthright from his brother. Jacob was a schemer, yet God still loved him and had chosen him. But God also knew he needed to be disciplined.

- God needed to show him that when you venture out into the world with nothing, *He is the One on whom you need to depend* (Proverbs 3:5). Trickery and deceit may work for a while with certain people, but it doesn't work too well when you're alone in the wild.
- God needed *to show the deceiver what it felt like to be deceived,* especially what it felt liked to be deceived out of something valuable and precious—in Jacob's case, the

wife he thought he was getting in exchange for seven years of labor.

- God needed to show him that *deceit leads to death and destruction* (the battle that might have been with Esau). Lying and deceit always leads your life into a downward spiral. At some point, repentance and restoration must occur.
- God needed to show him *the effects of unjust partiality* (his treatment of Leah versus Rachel) through the kidnapping of Joseph.

Jacob experienced these rebuking storms in the wilderness, through Laban's hands, through the confrontation with Esau, and through his sons' jealousy. His life seems a series of sad, unfortunate events.

Jacob's sanctifying journey
Genesis 47:9
*And Jacob said to Pharaoh, "The days of the years of my sojourning are 130 years. **Few and evil have been the days of the years of my life**, and they have not attained to the days of the years of the life of my fathers in the days of their sojourning."*

Jacob's days *do* seem few and evil. But, on closer examination, much of the evil that Jacob had to endure was *self-inflicted*. A continual series of poor choices led to poorer outcomes, and many of those outcomes seem to be God's rebukes through personal circumstances—trying to get Jacob to change and align his character and actions with God's.

Jacob's life is bittersweet for me. After everything he went through—the revelation of seeing angels ascending and descending into heaven, wrestling with the Pre-Incarnate Christ, and being given the name Israel (*"contender with God"*)—it's hard to see that Jacob *changed very much* during the course of his life. After God delivers him from Esau and they reconcile, he still is not honest with Esau when they depart. He still seems timid and cowardly after his daughter, Dinah, is raped. And he still plays favorites with Joseph, even though he should have known what it felt like to have *his* father treat him like an illegitimate stepchild. In short, it's hard to see that those rebuking storms God sent had much effect in his life at all.

Nevertheless, Jacob, like Peter, also gives us hope. Peter gives us hope that God can transform *anyone* into a leader of His Church. Jacob gives us

you are his wife. **How then can I do this great wickedness and sin against God?"**

Joseph didn't sleep with Potiphar's wife because it might jeopardize his "career." He chose not to sleep with her because *it was offensive to God*. Proud men usually don't care what God thinks, let alone whether God thinks *something is sin*.

Through the course of his trials, Joseph showed himself to be a God-fearing, humble man. He was entrusted with Potiphar's entire household (Genesis 39:1-5). He was entrusted with the running of the jail (Genesis 39:22-23). Both Potiphar and the head jailer had "...no concern..." about trusting Joseph with these responsibilities. It seems the reason Joseph is given this trust is because of his *character*, not necessarily his *competence*. I have known and know many competent men who are proud. Sooner or later, a man's lack of character catches up with whatever competence he has and exposes him for what he is—an untrustworthy man. That wasn't the case with Joseph.

What about parading his "coat of many colors" before his brothers? If you look back at the passage in Genesis mentioned at the beginning of this chapter, there is no mention of Joseph doing any such thing. Joseph was given a coat from his father to wear. *It honored his father* to wear that coat. What was he supposed to do, bury the coat in his knapsack and wear it for a few moments before he went to bed, just so he didn't tick off his brothers? Favoring Joseph was Jacob's fault. Joseph shouldn't be saddled with that. It was his brothers' hatred that was misdirected. For make no mistake about this: the object of his brothers' hate, whether they realized it or not, *was really Jacob, not Joseph.*

As far as his dreams were concerned, at best, we can say Joseph was naïve. He should have known his brothers hated him. Telling them his God-inspired dreams foretelling his eventual authority over them would only have added salt to their wounds.

At worst, Joseph may have been struggling with *revenge* not pride. For even though Joseph's brothers were the ones who felt like second-class citizens, it was likely *Joseph* who felt he was the true outcast. His brothers hated him. According to the narrative in Genesis 37, they could not even speak with him without being snide. He wanted to to have fellowship with his brothers but also needed to honor his father who wanted to make much of him. He wanted to be loved by his father, but not smothered in exclusivity at the cost of being ostracized by his brothers. *Joseph was in limbo between both his father and his brothers.*

It's not unreasonable—knowing Joseph's sin nature was no different than ours—that Joseph shared those dreams with them simply to say, "One day, things are going to change, fellas. I'm not always going to be your despicable little brother." If that was the issue, I would label his attitude more specifically as an issue of vengeance, not the catch-all phrase of "pride."

Joseph's sanctifying journey

That last point leads me to his storm of refinement. If the issue for Joseph was retribution or vengeance, then much of what he went through, looking over his life in total, seems to make sense. Here's why: Imagine for a moment a different biblical scenario. Joseph is somehow miraculously made "governor" of Canaan by Pharaoh at the tender age of seventeen. He has experienced the seething hatred of his brothers and, likely, their disdain for his father, all of his young life. If he were given the power to exile them or imprison them—for life—would he do it? Would you do it, knowing the level of maturity you had when you were seventeen, having experienced everything Joseph endured from his brothers? For some who have experienced child abuse or bullying in your family, either from a parent or from siblings, you know that question is a tough one to honestly answer.

Joseph needed to be cleansed and refined regarding this attitude toward his brothers. So the way God accomplished this was to have him be kidnapped by his brothers and sold into slavery? Then, when he thought life was at least tolerable and somewhat meaningful, he was thrown into prison for doing the right thing? And to top that off, when he was in prison and prophetically encouraged a man who was worried about his position with Pharaoh, the man forgot him—for two years? This was going to help his attitude of revenge toward his brothers?

Like most of our "smelting storms," the answer is yes. When we pray for patience, it seems God brings a multitude of things in our lives that cause us to be impatient. When we need to trust God for finances, it seems more bills come our way. An athlete is made stronger in the weight room by continually upping the weight of his reps. A runner gains more endurance by lengthening the distance of his runs. Joseph's "smelting storms" involved this same process. Issues and attitudes needed to be individually dealt with over time. All of them—in his case—involved trusting God as the One who exacts judgment and reward.

Proverbs 27:21 (Amplified Bible)
*As the refining pot for silver and the furnace for gold [bring forth all the impurities of the metal], so **let a man be in his trial of praise [ridding himself of all that is base or insincere**; for a man is judged by what he praises and of what he boasts].*

In all three episodes of his trials, Joseph was unjustly treated and was powerless to fight back. He had to depend on God's provision when what he had was taken from him. He had to hope in *God's* fairness regarding reward and punishment. And he had to have *patience* in trusting how God was going to take care of both of these issues in his life.

In that lonely trip to Egypt from Canaan, and in the dark dungeon of Pharaoh's prison, he learned to trust in God's justice, not his own. He experienced God's provision. He learned not to be bitter about the past (understanding that God is the One who controls our future) and proved it by his statement to his brothers (Genesis 50:19-20). It's a good thing he did learn those lessons, for if he had exacted all the pent-up rage that might have dwelt in his heart based on everything that happened to him on account of his brothers, *there may have been no Israel.* Think about that a minute: how critical was it—as far as long-term consequences were concerned—to have this character issue squared away in Joseph's life?

There are things God may be doing in your life right now that may seem exactly the opposite of what you think will help you. You may need money and yet more expenses are coming your way. You may need peace and yet your life is becoming more stressful. Just like you, I have scratched my head (usually it was more like screamed my head off) wondering what in the world God was doing in my life, when it seemed anyone could see that what I needed was—(fill in the blank. My needs probably weren't all that different from yours at one time or another).

God knows the right way to refine me. It usually is painful and stressful. It usually is something I would not wish on my worst enemy. But this is the work of sanctification, and from our perspective, these storms are usually messy—just like a smelting furnace. Like those furnaces, however, they also bring about permanent change.

3 NAOMI—THE STORM OF GLORIFYING GOD

Ruth 1:19-21

19 So the two of them went on until they came to Bethlehem. And when they to Bethlehem, the whole town was stirred because of them. And the women said, "Is this Naomi?" 20 She said to them, **"Do not call me Naomi [pleasant]; call me Mara [bitter], for the Almighty has dealt very bitterly with me.** *21 I went away full, and the* LORD *has brought me back empty. Why call me Naomi, when the* LORD *has testified against me and the Almighty has brought calamity upon me?"*

Naomi's storm is similar to the story of Mary and Lazarus (John 11) we discussed in *When God Disappoints*. But it's also very different (apart from the obvious fact that nobody rises from the dead.)

- There is a famine in Israel. Naomi, her husband and their two sons flee to Moab to escape the famine.

- Her husband dies in Moab.

- Her two sons take Moabite wives.

- After ten years, *both* her sons die.

- When she hears the LORD had "visited His people and given them food" (Ruth1:8), she determines to return to Israel.

- One daughter-in-law stays in Moab. The other (Ruth) is determined to stay with Naomi.

Ruth didn't have one tragedy like Mary. Her *life* up to this point seems like a tragedy. By her own testimony at the beginning of this chapter, she didn't think anything was pleasant about her life. It had been one tragedy after another, and she was bitter from it. If we could look up "Old Testament Woman Disappointed in God" in a Bible encyclopedia, we'd find a picture of Naomi.

God didn't raise her husband or sons from the dead, but He provided for Naomi through Ruth. When they re-enter Israel, Ruth gleans a field from sunrise to sunset, so she and Naomi can eat. It is back-breaking work that Naomi can't do. The owner of this field (Boaz, an older and wealthy man) is smitten with Ruth, for she is not only hard-working and bright, but she is also beautiful. Boaz and Ruth eventually marry and have a son, ensuring Naomi's long-term care.

God answered Naomi's immediate need: to provide for her sustenance, give her a companion (in Ruth), and give her a male heir (indirectly through Ruth and Boaz). But as I mentioned before, there was a hidden dollar bill on the floor. It was something she couldn't have seen even if she tried, for she was likely dead when her great, great grandson was born. That hidden dollar bill was David.

Why did her husband and sons have to die to accomplish this? Why was a Moabite woman needed to complete the lineage of David? I don't know. We could speculate on several things—as many have—but I think it's enough to make three simple observations from the story of Ruth and Naomi:

1) God promises to provide for His people, but the provision does not always come from a source we might expect. In this case, it was from a foreign believer. It was from a woman whom Naomi tried hard to shoo away, yet Ruth would not leave Naomi or Naomi's God. Sometimes God's provision is like that. It is the dollar bill on the ground that we think is not even worth picking up. Yet it is the very thing He has given to save and comfort us.

2) Tragedy *always* has purpose. Again, I don't know why her two sons had to die, but I do know this much by simply connecting the dots in Scripture: if Naomi's two sons hadn't died, then Boaz couldn't marry Ruth. If Boaz didn't marry Ruth, then he would have had no male heir. And if he had no male heir, then there would be no David, and the lineage of David would cease. That also means *the lineage of the Messiah would cease*. There are hidden dollar bills in tragedy that we will never see this side of heaven. We will talk more about tragedy and long-term outcomes later in this book.

3) God is glorified in this whole adventure. God gave new life to Naomi, adopted a Gentile into the lineage of Christ, showed favor to an older, single man by giving him a virtuous, beautiful wife, gave Israel its greatest mortal king, and gave the world its only true King and Savior. It all began with a famine in the land and a family that had to pack up and move.

I remember a pastor who wondered why I chose to study the Book of Ruth in a small group Bible study. His implication was that there wasn't enough "meat" in it for a small group discussion. I still disagree. Naomi's story is the story of us all, to one degree or another. It's a story that seems sadly ordinary, yet has a happy, simple ending. But it is a much bigger story than any of the players could have ever imagined. The same is true for you and me.

4 DANIEL—THE STORM OF SUFFERING FOR CHRIST

Daniel 6:10
*When Daniel **knew that the document had been signed,** he went to his house where he had windows in his upper chamber open toward Jerusalem. He got down on his knees three times a day and prayed and gave thanks before his God, **as he had done previously.***

Have you ever wondered, *"Why did Daniel go through with it?"* Perhaps my question seems odd to you. The "it" in my question is the evil scheme his enemies had planned for Daniel. The "go through with" is following the script they believed he would follow. Let me explain.

He knew, as the passage above states, that the document had been signed. *The* document was the edict Darius signed—rather, was tricked into

41

signing by Daniel's enemies—that anyone "who makes petition to any god or man for thirty days" except King Darius should be put to death (Daniel 6:7). I believe Daniel knew the king had been tricked, for he had established a close relationship with the king and knew the king's character. Daniel also knew the king trusted him and wanted to give him responsibility for the whole kingdom of Persia (Daniel 6:3).

So why play into his enemies hands? When faced with persecution, many believers over the centuries went underground. They did not stop practicing their faith. If caught, they did not deny or renounce their faith, but, in the meantime, they *did* lay low. Daniel could have easily done the same. And it would have only been for thirty days! But Daniel didn't do this. He did exactly what his enemies thought he would do and (knowingly) fell right into their trap.

So again I ask, *why did he go through with it*? I see two main reasons:

The cost of leadership
Matthew 10:25a
*"It is enough for **the disciple to be like his teacher**, and the servant like his master."*

John 13:16

*"Truly, truly, I say to you, **a servant is not greater than his master**, nor is a messenger greater than the one who sent him."*

Shadrach, Meshach, and Abednego—based on the chronology of the Book of Daniel—had already faced the threat of the fiery furnace. They would not bow down to Nebuchadnezzar's statue and told him so to his face. They did not go "underground" or find a way to avoid this confrontation. *They were willing to be burned alive* rather than publicly worship some pagan idol, and they showed this resolve in their actions. The question really isn't, "Why did Daniel go through with it?" The question should be, "How could Daniel *not* go through with it?"

Daniel was the leader of the four young men when they first arrived in Babylon. *He* was the one who took the initiative with the captain regarding the king's food. *He* was the one who was their leader regarding knowing and interpreting Nebuchadnezzar's dream—knowing he would likely be the first to be put to death if he got the interpretation of the dream wrong. *He set the example for them*, and they followed his example as their teacher when they were faced with a similar decision. It was now time—much later in

Daniel's life—for him to face a similar decision his "disciples" had already faced (and won), based on the faith they gained from Daniel's relationship with God. *How could Daniel not go through with it?*

John 13:12-16

¹² When he had washed their feet and put on his outer garments and resumed his place, he said to them, "Do you understand what I have done to you? ¹³ You call me Teacher and Lord, and you are right, for so I am. ¹⁴ If I then, your Lord and Teacher, have washed your feet, you also ought to wash one another's feet. **¹⁵ For I have given you an example, that you also should do just as I have done to you. ¹⁶ Truly, truly, I say to you, a servant is not greater than his master,** *nor is a messenger greater than the one who sent him.*

The Lord Jesus said that servants are not greater than their masters. He meant it in the context that His disciples should not think themselves above their Master (in hardship or lifestyle). But in the passage above, He also showed that a teacher isn't above his disciples. This passage is one of the reasons why "Do as I say, but not as I do" is such a wicked attitude for a teacher, parent or anyone in authority. It's not clear in the chronology of the Book of Daniel if any of Daniel's three friends were still alive at this time. Even if they weren't, Daniel was still their leader in his heart. He would face the lions just like they faced the furnace—regardless of what happened to him—and prove the godly resolve they learned from him was still there.

The cost of a godly lifestyle
2 Timothy 3:12
"*Indeed, **all who desire to live a godly life in Christ Jesus** will be persecuted...*"

2 Corinthians 2:15
*For we are the aroma of Christ to God **among those who are being saved and among those who are perishing...***

The opening passage I quoted at the beginning of this chapter also says that Daniel's "prayer routine" was something he had always done when he was in his house. It was why Daniel's enemies could so easily create their edict. They knew Daniel prayed three times a day because it was apparent and public knowledge to any believer or non-believer who cared to examine him. He was not pretentious about his faith. He didn't flout it in front of anyone's face, but he didn't change his lifestyle to suit his audience either.

Job 2:4
"Then Satan answered the LORD and said, "Skin for skin! All that a man has he will give for his life."

The Persian public might have thought the same thing Satan thought about Job if Daniel hadn't kept his public devotions. If Daniel didn't go through with it, all his praying, reading the Law, his proper speech and respect, his sexual purity and absence of other vices—in other words, being a true and faithful worshiper of the God of Israel— would seem to the Persians nothing more than a religion of hypocrisy. They would have thought the same of Daniel as Satan thought of Job: *when his life is on the line, he will cave.* Daniel "went through with it" because he knew he was not just an example to those he discipled, but also an example to the non-believing world. He was already a public figure who publically stood up for God in front of two kings. He would publically stand up again to a third king, regardless of the cost.

We are asked by Jesus to do the same. There will be times for escape and fight another day, as Paul did in Damascus and Jerusalem (Acts 9:23-25; 24:23-35). But even in those episodes, Paul's heart was what he expressed to the Caesareans in Acts 21:13 when he was told by the prophet Agabus that he would be imprisoned by the Jews:

Then Paul answered, "What are you doing, weeping and breaking my heart? **For I am ready not only to be imprisoned but even to die in Jerusalem for the name of the Lord Jesus.***"*

In this life, there will always be storms of suffering for endeavoring to live a godly life. At worst, I have suffered minor ridicule. I have never had to face a fiery furnace or a lion's den. Daniel's and his friends' stories had a happy ending, as far as their lives were concerned. Most believers' stories don't end happily in worldly terms. They're either tortured, scarred for life, or they die. Jesus said these storms were not just a possibility. He said they would come. I pray when that day comes, I will have Daniel's resolve.

DISAPPOINTMENT LEADS TO DEATH

1 Samuel 25:30-31a

^{30} "And when the L<small>ORD</small> has done to my lord according to all the good that he has spoken concerning you and has appointed you prince over Israel, ^{31} my lord shall have no cause of grief or pangs of conscience for having shed blood without cause or **for my lord working salvation himself**."

The words above are from Abigail. She prevented David from killing all of Nabal's men (and likely Nabal) when Nabal refused to give aid to David's men after they had watched over Nabal's shepherds in the fields. That last phrase of Abigail's is especially germane regarding the men and women we are about to examine. They chose to yield to their disappointment and bitterness in God and "work out their own salvation" *apart from God*. David working out his own salvation would have been through his and his men's swords and would have literally led to death.

The following five individuals' (or groups of individuals') actions didn't all immediately lead to violence, but they did all lead to death. It led to spiritual death in their relationship with God, death involving the immediate plans God had for them, and death involving their future.

Like Adam's and Eve's sin, their wrong choices set in motion a series of events that brought about evil over many years to come. Cain, Lot's daughters, Rebekah, Joseph's brothers, and Saul all yielded to the temptation to work out their problems and disappointments apart from God. Each has an example for us regarding being disappointed in God.

We'll begin with Cain and his disappointment in God's discipline.

5 CAIN—REJECTING GOD'S DISCIPLINE

Genesis 4:1-6

*Now Adam knew Eve his wife, and she conceived and bore Cain, saying, "I have gotten a man with the help of the LORD." ² And again, she bore his brother Abel. Now Abel was a keeper of sheep, and Cain a worker of the ground. ³ **In the course of time Cain brought to the LORD an offering of the fruit of the ground, ⁴** and Abel also brought of the firstborn of his flock and of their fat portions. And the LORD had regard for Abel and his offering, ⁵ **but for Cain and his offering he had no regard.***

*** So Cain was very angry, and his face fell. ⁶ The LORD said to Cain, "Why are you angry, and why has your face fallen? ⁷ If you do well, will you not be accepted?** And if you do not do well, sin is* *crouching at the door. Its desire is for you, but you must rule over it."*

The Bible doesn't give a lot of commentary about Cain. It tells us his deeds were evil—*before* he murdered Abel (1 John 3:12)—implying the unacceptable sacrifice of fruits and vegetables he offered to the LORD was not just a simple mistake. It was because Cain didn't want to give a sacrifice that cost him anything. The Bible also tells us that Abel offered his sacrifice in faith (Hebrews 11:4). It was likely the kind of faith that said, "What I have will never be enough to be right with You. What I give, I give in humility, trusting in Your mercy." If Abel offered his sacrifice in faith, and it was accepted, then it stands to reason that Cain *didn't* offer his sacrifice in faith. His was an attitude that may have said, "This is what I owe You. Period."

It may sound nonsensical, but as far as our discussion is concerned, *what* Cain didn't do to gain God's approval is not as important as *how* he reacted to God's disapproval. God let Cain know in unmistakable terms that what he had done was wrong. God also let him know in unmistakable terms that if Cain changed, he would be approved and accepted by God. It wasn't a one-strike-and-you're-out issue. It wasn't even a three-strike policy. God would have been as patient with Cain as He was with Jacob, and Jacob's journey was a lifelong lesson in learning the right way to walk with God.

No, the issue was *how* Cain handled God's discipline. He reacted with anger and resentment. He obviously felt that he wasn't the problem. In his mind, *Abel* was the problem. *Abel* was the one who was obviously keeping him from being approved by God. If there was no Abel to be compared to, then Cain's standards of righteousness would be the norm and everything would fall neatly into place.

We will see this theme over and over in our character studies: When examining our problems, *all roads ultimately lead back to God. God* was Cain's problem, not Abel. But how do you fight back against God? You can't. With what will you hurt God? Nothing—He is self-sufficient and invincible. So Cain vented his displeasure against God with someone who was a friend of God's: his brother Abel.

It's easy to judge Cain. The problem seems so obvious; the solution, so simple. God says stop what you're doing and do it another way—His way. You say, "Okay, Lord. Show me how I can change and help me do it." Of course, it rarely happens that way. What usually happens is we become frustrated when what *we* think is right is judged to be wrong. We get frustrated when the direction we believe is the right path is judged to be wrong. And so we fight back.

The fight may not manifest itself in murder. It may manifest itself in adultery or some other lust. It may manifest itself in some form of escapism, whether it is something dark like drugs or pornography, or something seemingly harmless like work or sports. Regardless what form it takes, a person who has been rebuked by God, either through His written Word, through some individual, or through circumstances—and rejects God's correction—is very often angry at God. Like Cain, they may not consciously be aware of it, let alone acknowledge it, but God is the source of their anger.

If not dealt with correctly, being rebuked by God can lead to rebellion, isolation, and death. The story of Cain and Abel is really a tragic story of two deaths—the physical death of Abel and the spiritual death of Cain. This anger, as the story of Cain shows us, destroys. It destroyed his brother's life, his parents' lives, and ultimately his life—for he was exiled from the two living people who truly cared about him.

The life of Cain is one reason why the Psalms and Proverbs are filled with warnings to accept rebuke and correction *and learn from it, not fight against it.*

Psalms 94:12
"Blessed is the man whom you discipline, O LORD, and whom you teach out of your law..."*

Psalms 141:5
*Let a righteous man strike me—it is a kindness; **let him rebuke me—it is oil for my head;** let my head not refuse it.*

Proverbs 6:23
*"For the commandment is a lamp and the teaching a light, and **the reproofs of discipline are the way of life**..."*

No one likes to be corrected, let alone rebuked. The passages above appeal to our reason—not our emotions—to listen and repent in the face of God's corrections. It's always simpler to say this than to do it, for even Scripture acknowledges that corrective discipline never feels "good." *It always feels painful.* (Hebrews 12:11).

When I look back over my Christian life, I realize many of the times I was irritable or short with people had nothing to do with the person I was dealing with or the circumstances I was in. It was because I knew there was something in my life that God showed me I needed to change—something I knew was wrong—but I didn't want to repent. The tension and anger I felt was really directed at God. Maybe this is a source of bitterness and disappointment in your life, as well.

Cain's story is also a story of grace. God did punish him, but He also protected him. It was *Cain* who "fled from the presence of the LORD." God didn't push him away (Genesis 4:16). God doesn't want us to run away from Him either. As our Father, He wants us to lean on Him during these corrections, knowing the eventual outcome will always be for our good.

6 REBEKAH—IMPATIENCE IN GOD'S PROMISE

Genesis 25:21-23; 27-28

²¹ And Isaac prayed to the LORD for his wife, because she was barren. And the LORD granted his prayer, and Rebekah his wife conceived. ²² The children struggled together within her, and she said, "If it is thus, why is this happening to me?" So she went to inquire of the LORD. ²³ And the LORD said to her, "Two nations are in your womb, and two peoples from within you shall be divided; **the one shall be stronger than the other, the older shall serve the younger.***"*
²⁷ When the boys grew up, Esau was a skillful hunter, a man of the field, while Jacob was a quiet

man, dwelling in tents. [28] ***Isaac loved Esau because he ate of his game, but Rebekah loved Jacob.***

God gave Rebekah a prophecy regarding the twins that were in her womb. To Rebekah, it was more than a prophecy, it was a promise. It was a promise that the child she dearly loved would eventually be stronger and more successful than her other "difficult" child. Esau was more than the simple narrative described in verse twenty-eight. He was not a man who was spiritual or even reflective (Genesis 25:29-34). He married two Hittite women—likely against the advice of Isaac and Rebekah—and they made Rebekah's life miserable (Genesis 26:34-35). In short, if Rebekah had a daughter and Esau was a neighbor boy who came to ask her daughter out on a date, Rebekah would have flatly said, "No."

But she had hope. For God had said that her other son, the quiet and reflective one, would actually rule the older one. So she waited for the fulfillment of God's prophecy. But when the time came for the blessing by her husband of the chosen one, something had gone terribly wrong. Jacob had likely already told Rebekah about the incident where Esau sold his birthright for a single meal. She knew Esau was a man of little character, but her husband was old now and he didn't see Esau the way she saw him. Isaac was fully prepared to give Esau the birthright he didn't deserve. God's plan was going to crash before it even got off the ground! *So she took matters into her own hands.* And though she thought she had solved her problems, this is where all of Jacob's problems began.

Rebekah decided to "help" God's plan by devising a scheme to trick Isaac into blessing Jacob. She made lamb taste like wild game. She put Esau's best garments on Jacob. She placed woolly skins on his hands and neck to imitate Esau's hairiness. As we discussed, Jacob means "deceiver" or "supplanter," but Rebekah did a pretty good job of being a deceiver herself. Think about this a minute: to fulfill God's plan for her (and her son's) life, she believed she had to deceive her husband and make her son lie to his father.

Rebekah faltered because she didn't trust that God could and would fulfill His promise *His* way. That "way" may have not been clear to her, but there is one thing she should have kept in mind: *God never asks us to break one of His laws to fulfill another.* Unfortunately, Rebekah didn't wait for the Lord to see how He would fulfill this seemingly impossible promise. She took matters into her own hands. Did God work through the sad chain of events that followed? Absolutely. But that still doesn't excuse what Rebekah did.

What's so surprising about Rebekah is she had already seen God grant an amazing answer to prayer in her life. (She conceived twins when she was barren.) She had also heard about the birth of her husband, which was a promise that God fulfilled to Abraham and Sarah when they were as good as dead (Hebrews 11:11-12). So why not trust God now?

Rebekah's problem is an issue all Christians face. We believe God has given us a promise. We are sure He will grant what He has told us. But over time, nothing seems to be happening. In fact, based on our present circumstances, the promise He has given seems so unlikely to happen, we soon arrive at a three-pronged road of temptation.

The road of doubt

The road of doubt leads you to believe that you were never right about what you heard from God in the first place. You were just presumptuous in your faith. What you read in your devotion, what you believed you heard God speaking to you in your conscience was just you—just wishful thinking. You don't blame God for your misstep, it was just bad judgment on your part.

The problem with going down this road is that you become less confident about *any* personal application God gives you in His Word. Going down this path also causes you to question other promises you believe God has given you in the past. Maybe those were just episodes of wishful thinking, too. Even if those promises were "fulfilled," maybe they really weren't fulfilled at all. Maybe they were just amazing, fortuitous events—things to be thankful for, but not fulfilled promises.

The road of bitterness

The road of bitterness leads you to believe you *were* right about what you heard from God. So *God* must be wrong because what He promised isn't being fulfilled. You waited and waited for God to come through and He didn't—plain and simple. While others may try to explain why something didn't happen (yet) in your life, it just sounds like a bad used car salesman trying to explain away why the car that won't run right really just needs to be broken in a little bit more.

Of course, the problem with going down this road is what we spoke of in chapter three of *When God Disappoints.* This road leads to spiritual death. For if God was wrong about this particular promise in your life, then maybe all those promises that are found in the Bible regarding His Word, Himself, and salvation are also questionable. If those things are questionable, then your Christian faith is a lie and you are a fraud if you continue to believe it.

The road of self-salvation

This was Rebekah's road. She knew God had given her a promise, but, in her mind, the promise was in danger of not being fulfilled. Things were happening that were not supposed to be happening in her view, and it seemed God was caught off guard by them. So she would fulfill the promise with the attitude of, "If it has to be, then it must be me."

The problem with working out our salvation this way is that it is done without faith, which isn't pleasing to God (Hebrews 11:6). It's done without selflessness, which only leads to chaos and strife (James 3:14-17). And it's done without God— without His input and direction—and this usually leads to death and futility (Psalm 127:1; Proverbs 14:12).

Psalm 37:7-9

Be still before the LORD and wait patiently for him; *fret not yourself over the one who prospers in his way, over the man who carries out evil devices!* *⁸ Refrain from anger, and forsake wrath! Fret not yourself; it tends only to evil. ⁹ For the evildoers* *shall be cut off,* **but those who wait for the L**ORD **shall inherit the land.**

The other road is the road Scripture repeatedly tells us to take. That road is called "Wait for the Lord." Even if it makes no sense at all, even if your wait is much longer than you thought it should reasonably be, wait for the Lord. Are you in the middle of a promise that seems to be going nowhere (or maybe even going *backwards*)? So was Rebekah. She needed to wait and see how God would "play out His hand" in the matter. You and I need to do the same.

7 LOT'S DAUGHTERS—THE DARK FUTURE

Genesis 19:30-38

*30 Now Lot went up out of Zoar and lived in the hills with his two daughters, for he was afraid to live in Zoar. So he lived in a cave with his two daughters. 31 And the firstborn said to the younger, "Our father is old, **and there is not a man on earth to come in to us after the manner of all the earth**. 32 Come, let us make our father drink wine, and we will lie with him, **that we may preserve offspring from our father."** 33 So they made their father drink wine that night. And the firstborn went in and lay with her father. He did not know when she lay down or when she arose.*

34 The next day, the firstborn said to the younger, "Behold, I lay last night with my father. Let us make him drink wine tonight also. Then you go in and lie with him, that we may preserve offspring from our father." [35] So they made their father drink wine that night also. And the younger arose and lay with him, and he did not know when she lay down or when she arose. [36] Thus both the daughters of Lot became pregnant by their father. [37] The firstborn bore a son and called his name Moab. **He is the father of the Moabites to this day.** *[38] The younger also bore a son and called his name Ben-ammi.* **He is the father of the Ammonites to this day.**

Two sisters were engaged the night before their lives changed forever. They both shared the hope of a husband, children, and building a life in a pleasant valley. The people weren't that nice, but sometimes you have to take the good with the bad. Then something very disturbing happened to their family. Two "men" who said they were sent from God told them their city would be destroyed. They told these sisters and their mom and dad that they needed to leave that night.

Their dad tried to get their fiancés to leave the city as well, but their fiancés ignored him. The "men" persistently urged them to leave immediately, but it was the middle of the night, and what was the big hurry? Would the men of the city who tried to attack the house come back again? Everything seemed so muddled. Finally, they and their father and mother left the city, literally dragged by the hands of those two "men."

As dawn broke, they saw, heard, and smelled fire like they had never seen or imagined before, raining down in torrents on their city and valley. It instantly consumed everything it fell on. Their mother lingered; a step forward, then two steps back. Then a half step forward and three steps back. Before long, she was closer to the growing conflagration of fire and sulfur then she was to her daughters and husband. To their horror, she was eventually consumed by the heat and sulfur. At last, they found a cave to rest and regroup. In twenty-four hours they had experienced an unbelievable journey into the surreal and the horrifying.

After a few days, they assessed their situation: their mother was dead, their fiancés were dead, and the town they had lived in—no, in fact, the whole valley—now resembled a picture of hell more than a picture of anything that might exist on earth. Their father was afraid to venture into the only remaining town near the valley, perhaps because he felt the residents would blame him (as the foreign resident who believed in the foreign

God) for the catastrophe that happened up the road.

In these sisters' minds, there was nothing before them but darkness. There seemed to be no hope of finding a man to marry. They were all *dead*. Their father was too scared to venture out into the surrounding towns. So it seemed their destiny was to live in a cave—alone—for the rest of their lives.

But there was one man who could give them children so they would not be alone. It was their father, Lot. They got him drunk so he would not be aware of what they were doing. They both became pregnant and were the mothers of two nations. Lot's daughters are never mentioned by name in Scripture. The infamy of their deed is enough to remember them.

What they did was despicable. But we should be fair in our condemnation--many others have faced a future that also looked completely dark and made similarly poor choices, with equally disastrous results. Unlike Rebekah, these young women had no specific promises. In fact, their lives resemble Naomi's more than Rebekah's—only worse. Not only were their mother and fiancés dead, their town was "dead." They likely saw the horrific firestorm raining down from heaven on their valley. This probably made an indelible image in their minds regarding the character of God, one that shaped their future actions.

They barely escaped with their lives. Their mother dawdled and didn't. What did God spare them for? So they could live happily in a cave—alone—for the rest of their lives? "Thanks so much for looking out for us God. Next time, just let us die with everyone else. It would have been more humane."

There are many who can relate to these women's dark future. You may be one. To you, the future may seem foreboding because of the recent disaster from which you came. You may feel bruised, breathless, and frightened. You may wonder where God was in your ordeal and wonder how He could be anywhere in the dark future that stands before you. It seems obvious, based on your circumstances, that God can't be trusted. And you are tempted—like Lot's daughters, like Rebekah—to take matters into your own hands.

The choice made by Rebekah and Lot's daughters in the face of a dark future was similar. But here is the difference: Rebekah had been given a promise years ago—an unusual, specific, prophetic promise—about her beloved Jacob. She needed to believe that the same God who promised a child to her mother-in-law when she was well past child-bearing age and fulfilled it, could also fulfill a promise to her that seemed unlikely. She needed to believe what God *had said*, in spite of the contrary circumstances that confronted her.

The issue for Lot's daughters was that they weren't truly aware of what God *was saying* in their dark circumstances. God showed them a clear picture of their worth (and God's mercy) through the angels' words and actions. Let's review the events of that night and what the angels told these daughters, realizing that angels can only say and do what *God* instructs them to say and do.

Genesis 19:4-5
*4 But before they lay down, the men of the city, the men of Sodom, both young and old, **all the people to the last man**, surrounded the house. 5 And they called to Lot, "Where are the men who came to you tonight? Bring them out to us, that we may know them."*

"All the people to the last man" means every man—*including the fiancés of Lot's daughters.* They, too, were in front of Lot's house, demanding to sodomize the two angels. Yet the angels still asked if there was anyone (sons-in-law, daughters-in-law, etc.) whom they might save from the wrath that was coming on the city (Genesis 19:12-13), also including Lot's daughters' fiancés. What the daughters missed was God's grace in overlooking the sins of their fiancés. Those men would have been allowed to be saved, in spite of their behavior. They chose not to listen.

Genesis 19:15-16
¹⁵ *As morning dawned, the angels urged Lot, saying, "Up! Take your wife and your two daughters who are here, lest you be swept away in the punishment of the city."* ¹⁶ *But he lingered.* **So the men seized him and his wife and his two daughters by the hand, the LORD being merciful to him, and they brought him out and set him outside the city.**

God would have been perfectly justified to tell Lot's family of the coming disaster and, if they lingered (which implied they *wanted* to stay), destroy the city with them in it. They had been urgently warned and had ignored the warning. What more was God supposed to do? Drag them out of the city, that's what. God did not just show mercy towards them, He showed *He loved them* and was not going to let them decide their fate. Apparently, they did not truly believe God's warnings because staying would have meant death.

Genesis 19:22
[22] *"Escape there quickly, **for I can do nothing** till you arrive there."*

Lot had asked that they not have to travel so far to escape the wrath that was coming. God granted his request to escape to a nearby town. God made it clear through the angels' words that *their safety was His highest priority*. The judgment would not start until they were out of harm's way.

Lot's daughters missed all these messages of long-suffering, grace, mercy, and love. If they had truly heard and remembered them, the dark future they faced wouldn't have seemed so dark. The dots would have been easier to connect regarding God's character. Since God had been so incredibly patient with them regarding their deliverance from such a catastrophe, surely He would protect them as they ventured out into an unknown future.

If they had just stopped and thought about what had just transpired, God wouldn't have seemed like a swift, unpredictable avenger of death, but a merciful Shepherd who had protected them and would give them a future and a hope (Jeremiah 29:11).

They didn't connect the dots. In unbelief and fear, they chose to work out their own salvation apart from God. The epilogue of their story in Genesis 19:37-38 is not subtle. It is meant to show us the far-reaching effects of acting in faithless bitterness. The sons of Lot's daughters became the nations of the Moabites and the Ammonites. Those nations were enemies of Israel for centuries; their judgment was eternal.

Deuteronomy 23:3-4
³ "**No Ammonite or Moabite** may enter the assembly of the LORD. Even to the tenth generation, **none of them may enter the assembly of the LORD forever**, ⁴ because they did not meet you with bread and with water on the way, when you came out of Egypt, and because they hired against you Balaam the son of Beor from Pethor of Mesopotamia, to curse you."

Zephaniah 2:9
"Therefore, as I live," declares the Lord of hosts, the God of Israel, "**Moab shall become like Sodom, and the Ammonites like Gomorrah**, a land possessed by nettles and salt pits, and a waste forever. The remnant of my people shall plunder them, and the survivors of my nation shall possess them."

But even through all the evil and judgments that came from the acts of Lot's daughters, God was still merciful. For as we have already seen, there was one Moabite who would be beloved in Israel and would be part of the lineage of the Christ. Her name was Ruth.

8 JOSEPH'S BROTHERS—THE TROUBLED HOME

Genesis 29:31-35

31 **When the L**ORD **saw that Leah was hated, he opened her womb,** *but Rachel was barren.* *32* *And Leah conceived and bore a son, and she called his name Reuben, for she said,* **"Because the L**ORD **has looked upon my affliction; for now my husband will love me."** *33* *She conceived again and bore a son, and said,* **"Because the L**ORD **has heard that I am hated, he has given me this son also."** *And she called his name Simeon.* *34* *Again she conceived and bore a son, and said,* **"Now this time my husband will be attached to me,** *because I have borne him three sons." Therefore his name was called Levi.* *35* *And she conceived again and bore a son, and said, "This time I will praise the L*ORD.*" Therefore* *she called his name Judah. Then she ceased bearing.*

Genesis 31:14
*¹⁴ In the days of wheat harvest Reuben went and found mandrakes in the field and brought them to his mother Leah. Then Rachel said to Leah, "Please give me some of your son's mandrakes." ¹⁵ But she said to her, "**Is it a small matter that you have taken away my husband**? Would you take away my son's mandrakes also?"*

Bearing six sons for Jacob didn't endear Leah to him. She was still "the other woman" in Jacob's mind. She was the object of a cruel trick that was played on him. Therefore, she was someone to be forgotten and ignored. Reuben, Simeon, Levi, Judah (and later Issachar and Zebulun) had to have noticed this, just like any child would have noticed it. Because their father ignored their mother, it was likely they were ignored, too, since the primary object of their father's love was their mother's sister and her two children.

When you look at this family that way, it's not hard to see why Leah's sons despised Joseph. Whenever they saw him with Jacob, Joseph represented everything they wanted from their father but were not given. Every time they looked into Joseph's face they saw Rachel, the woman who made their mother sad and lonely for the affectionate touch of their father. Year after agonizing year this went on. It's not shocking to me that they conspired to get rid of Joseph. Based on their home life, it is amazing to me that, apart from God's grace, they didn't try to kill Joseph sooner.

I mentioned in chapter two that these brothers weren't attacking Joseph. The person they were really attacking was Jacob, whether they knew it or not. Digging even deeper, their sin was much like Cain's. The *object* of their bitterness wasn't Jacob, it was God. As I said before, *all roads lead back to God*. Why did *God* permit their father to ignore their mother? Why didn't *God* cause Jacob to care more about them?

There are many men and women who struggle with similar types of questions long after their mothers and fathers are dead. Like Cain, Joseph's brothers couldn't do anything to God, and they wouldn't do anything to their father. *Joseph* was the natural choice on whom they could vent their bitterness and anger, so they sold him into slavery. No more Joseph, no more Jacob doting over Rachel's child, and they and their mother would finally take their rightful place in their father's eyes.

Of course, it was the wrong choice, the wrong path for them to take. What *do* you do when you are in a household where injustice is a normal way of life? If you are a child or a woman who feels threatened (either physically or sexually), you seek outside help and (ideally) remove yourself from the home. But what if it is a situation like Joseph's brother experienced? Their situation is shaded gray more than stark black and white, just like it is for many Christians.

I don't pretend to have an all-purpose answer regarding this kind of family conflict, but there is one example that comes to mind--that example is Hannah.

1 Samuel 1:4-7; 10-11

⁴ On the day when Elkanah sacrificed, he would give portions to Peninnah his wife and to all her sons and daughters. ⁵ But to Hannah he gave a double portion, because he loved her, though the Lᴏʀᴅ had closed her womb. **⁶ And her rival used to provoke her grievously to irritate her,** *because the Lᴏʀᴅ had closed her womb.* **⁷ So it went on year by year.** *As often as she went up to the house of the Lᴏʀᴅ,* **she used to provoke her. Therefore Hannah wept and would not eat...**

¹⁰ She was deeply distressed and prayed to the Lᴏʀᴅ and wept bitterly. *¹¹ And she vowed a vow* *and said, "O LORD of hosts, if you will indeed look on the affliction of your servant and remember me and not forget your servant, but will give to your servant a son,* **then I will give him to the LORD all the days of his life,** *and no razor shall touch his head."*

There are three things I see in this passage:

Don't retaliate

Hannah's distressful family situation went on year after year. She wept a lot. She did not eat. But she did not retaliate against Peninnah. She could have. 1 Samuel 1:3 makes it clear Hannah was loved more than Peninnah by Elkinah. She could have turned to her husband and said something like, "Look, since you aren't going to make Peninnah stop yammering at me, I'll make her stop—permanently." What she did was obey what was written of Christ in 1 Peter 2:23:

[23] When he was reviled, he did not revile in return; when he suffered, he did not threaten, but continued entrusting himself to him who judges justly.

Earnestly pray

Hannah recognized only God could truly deliver her from her troubles. It would have to be on His terms, in His time. That didn't mean she had a fatalistic attitude regarding her life and troubles. She wept aloud and prayed. She mouthed her requests, weeping softly as she prayed. And like the Lord Jesus, she was heard for her godly reverence.

Hebrews 5:7
7 In the days of his flesh, Jesus offered up prayers and supplications, with loud cries and tears, to him who was able to save him from death, and he was heard because of his reverence.

Seek God's glory

The moral of Hannah receiving a son isn't, "Make a vow to God and commit yourself to follow through with it, and He will grant your request." Hannah's vow was really a request that said, "Let this—whatever "this" is—glorify You, Lord." And God *was* glorified. Samuel was one of the greatest prophets and priests of the Old Testament.

I know; it's easier said than done. For even when we do what is right, the ending isn't always so neat and tidy like Hannah's. We will examine another individual later in this book who didn't take up the sword in family strife. Her life didn't have a happy ending. Yet God still honored the choices she made.

9 SAUL—THE TRAP OF FAME

1 Samuel 18:6-9

*⁶ As they were coming home, when David returned from striking down the Philistine, the women came out of all the cities of Israel, singing and dancing, to meet King Saul, with tambourines, with songs of joy, and with musical instruments. ⁷ And the women sang to one another as they celebrated, "Saul has struck down his thousands, and David his ten thousands." ⁸ And Saul was very angry, and this saying displeased him. He said, **"They have ascribed to David ten thousands, and to me they have ascribed thousands, and what more can he have but the kingdom?" ⁹ And Saul eyed David from that day on.***

There are many aspects of Saul's life we could dissect that would offer insights into how we are not to live our Christian lives. Regarding being disappointed in God, the biggest issue Saul had was his relentless clinging to the kingship that God had taken away from him. Samuel had already told Saul that God had rejected him as king over Israel. He even further made the point clear to Saul by way of illustration (when Saul clung to Samuel's robe and it tore away) that Saul's kingdom had been torn from him (1 Samuel 16:23-28).

From a dispassionate, biblically-logical stance, it would seem what Saul should have thought to himself was, "I blew it. I wanted to be king, but God knows best. Hopefully the next king will be better than me. If God needs me to help the next king in some way, I'll make myself available." To be fair to Saul, that ideal rarely happens with *any* Christian—even a committed, mature Christian—when some position or authority is taken away. Whether it was because of sin or incompetence on our part, or because someone better qualified was found to replace us, it is difficult to release our grip on authority and fame.

Power has its privileges and fame fuels our egos. Of all the character flaws Saul had (and there were several), this one stands out the most—he would not let go of position and fame. It set him against his son, it drove him to murder, and it drove him to sorcery. It's ironic that this was his downfall. When he was first chosen as king of Israel, Saul was humble and afraid of the position (1 Samuel 9:20-21; 10:21-22). God worked through his humility and Saul began his reign as a fearless and humble leader (1 Samuel 11:12-15). What changed Saul?

Saul forgot who he used to be

2 Samuel 7:8-9; 18

*8 Now, therefore, thus you shall say to my servant David, 'Thus says the LORD of hosts, **I took you from the pasture, from following the sheep, that you should be prince over my people Israel.** 9 And I have been with you wherever you went and have cut off all your enemies from before you...*

*...18 Then King David went in and sat before the LORD and said, "**Who am I, O Lord GOD, and what is my house, that you have brought me thus far?***

David never forgot where he came from. God made him a valiant warrior, a prophet, and a wise king. But in his heart, David remembered he was only a shepherd boy, someone who desperately needed God's help and direction. David never acted like the "big man on campus," and apart from his sin against Uriah the Hittite, he did not abuse his power and fame as king.

Saul forgot where power and fame come from
Matthew 3:4-6
⁴ *Now John wore a garment of camel's hair and a leather belt around his waist, and his food was locusts and wild honey.* ⁵ ***Then Jerusalem and all Judea and all the region about the Jordan were going out to him,*** ⁶ *and they were baptized by him in the river Jordan, confessing their sins.*

John 3:27-28; 30
²⁷ *John answered,* ***"A person cannot receive even one thing unless it is given him from heaven.*** ²⁸ *You yourselves bear me witness, that I said, 'I am not the Christ, but I have been sent before him…*
*…³⁰ **He must increase, but I must decrease.***"

John the Baptist understood this principle. Think about this for a moment: most everyone in Israel at that time knew about John. If you were *anyone* spiritual—apart from the Pharisees—the "in" place to be was at the Jordan to seek out John. John had fame, he was held in great honor, and while he didn't have the power to grant life or death, he was still very influential.

Yet John knew he wasn't in control of any of this in his life. The context of John's quote in the passage above (regarding receiving anything from

God) was in relation to position and fame. Any day, at any moment, another One would come, and John's fame and influence would be gone. That was fine with him. *He knew he never owned it in the first place.*

Saul forgot about the results of pride
Proverbs 29:23
"***One's pride will bring him low****, but he who is lowly in spirit will obtain honor."*

2 Chronicles 32:25
[25] But Hezekiah did not make return according to the benefit done to him, for his heart was proud. ***Therefore wrath came upon him and Judah and Jerusalem.***

Ezekiel 28:17
"Your heart was proud because of your beauty; you corrupted your wisdom for the sake of your splendor. ***I cast you to the ground; I exposed you before kings****, to feast their eyes on you."*

The Bible mentions "pride" or "proud" 94 times regarding human behavior. None of the results are good. Pride is evil because it puts me above others. When pride characterizes my life, I justify any evil because I am worth it. But pride's greater evil is that it sets me above God. It tells me my plans and desires are more important than God's. It tells me my way of doing things is the right way. If God's plans match up with mine, well and good. But if not, my plans and the execution of those plans will always trump God's ways and plans.

Saul forgot all these things. He relentlessly tried to keep his fame and position, and the results were disastrous. You and I need to have the same perspective David and John the Baptist had regarding position and fame. All power and authority belong to God (Psalm 62:11). He is the only one who can cause someone to use it correctly because within our sinful frames, power and fame will destroy us.

DISAPPOINTMENT AND SELFISH AMBITION

1 Kings 3:5
*At Gibeon the LORD appeared to Solomon in a dream by night, and God said, "**Ask what I shall give you.**"*

The Lord knows we have deep desires and aspirations in our hearts. You may not have had *God ask you* the question above regarding your dreams and ambitions, but doubtless *you have asked Him* to grant your deepest desires many times. I have, too. Sometimes those desires have been granted, but most of the time, the answer has been "wait." As I mentioned in *When God Disappoints*, when these desires—these "selfish ambitions"—are not granted, it can lead to bitterness and disappointment in God.

I also mentioned three reasons why our desires may not be granted when we think they should:

It's not yet God's acceptable time
2 Corinthians 6:2 (NASB)

… *for He says, "AT THE ACCEPTABLE TIME I LISTENED TO YOU, AND ON THE DAY OF SALVATION I HELPED YOU."*

God is still "setting the stage"
Genesis 15:13-16

*¹³ Then the LORD said to Abram, "Know for certain that your offspring will be sojourners in a land that is not theirs and will be servants there, and they will be afflicted for four hundred years. ¹⁴ **But I will bring judgment on the nation that they serve,** and afterward they shall come out with great possessions. ¹⁵ As for you, you shall go to your fathers in peace; you shall be buried in a good old age. ¹⁶ And they shall come back here in the fourth generation, **for the iniquity of the Amorites is not yet complete."***

We're not mature enough in Christ to handle it
Hebrews 5:14

*But **solid food is for the mature**, for those who have their powers of discernment **trained by constant practice** to distinguish good from evil.*

We'll examine three individuals whose lives were an example of why desires and ambitions in our lives are not granted by God the way we think they should.

The first individual is Mary, the mother of Jesus. From our perspective, hers is one of the more puzzling reasons, because there wasn't a clear "why" regarding the granting of her request. From God's perspective, the timing simply wasn't right. It didn't mean it wouldn't happen. It just meant, "Not now."

10 MARY—THE UNACCEPTABLE TIME

Luke 1:26-36

*26 In the sixth month the angel Gabriel was sent from God to city of Galilee named Nazareth, 27 to a virgin betrothed to a man whose name was Joseph, of the house of David. And the virgin's name was Mary. 28 And he came to her and said, "Greetings, O favored one, the Lord is with you!" 29 But she was greatly troubled at the saying, and tried to discern what sort of greeting this might be. 30 And the angel said to her, "Do not be afraid, Mary, for you have found favor with God. 31 **And behold, you will conceive in your womb and bear a son, and you shall call his name Jesus. 32 He will be great and will be called the Son of the Most High. And the Lord God will give to him the throne of his father***

David, [33] and he will reign over the house of Jacob forever, and of his kingdom there will be no end."[34] And Mary said to the angel, "How will this be, since I am a virgin?" [35] And the angel answered her, "The Holy Spirit will come upon you, and the power of the Most High will overshadow you; therefore the child to be born will be called holy— the Son of God.

You remember the narrative of the birth of the Lord Jesus. While it was a dazzling and awe-inspiring advent for the shepherds in the field, it was anything but inspiring for Mary. She was forced to travel to Bethlehem late in her pregnancy. When the time came for her promised Son to be delivered, she likely delivered Him in a musty cave of a stall and had to place Him in a feeding trough for His bed. However, what you may not think about when you remember this story is the trial Mary had to endure *before* her journey to Bethlehem.

During her pregnancy, there were likely lots of sideways glances and hushed whispers. "She's pregnant, but Joseph isn't the father? Then who *is* the father? Oh, I see—it was the *Holy Spirit* that caused her to be pregnant. Yes, of course, dear; that makes *perfect* sense." And with rolled eyes or judgmental scowls, the women who knew Mary would walk away. There were some hopeful signs for Mary that buoyed her spirits and helped her faith regarding the promise she had been given: the shepherds' testimony on the night of His birth, the wise men from the East who visited her home with gifts for a King, and the young lad Jesus who astonished the rabbis with his teaching in the Temple. All of these things she "...*treasured in her heart, pondering what they might mean* (Luke 2:20).

But even as Jesus was growing up, there was no obvious sign that He was the Messiah. He was obedient to His parents and found favor with God and men (Luke 2:52). That could describe lots of boys and girls, as well as young men and women. That in itself wasn't any kind of confirming sign for Mary or the people. I'm sure Jesus bore their sideways glances and whispers as He was growing up as well, but this application is about Mary.

Her sadness and frustration came not just from the comments she endured regarding her Son, but also regarding her own integrity. What she had said to her doubters was true. Few likely believed her. She knew one day her Son would show them. One day, she would be vindicated, and the mouths of all those slanderers would be permanently shut.

When would that day be? How long would she have to wait? Thirty years? No, it was—and will be—longer than that. But one day there was a marriage feast in nearby Cana.

John 2:1-5

On the third day there was a wedding at Cana in Galilee, and the mother of Jesus was there. ²Jesus also was invited to the wedding with his disciples. **³ When the wine ran out, the mother of Jesus said to him, "They have no wine." ⁴ And Jesus said to her, "Woman, what does this have to do with me? My hour has not yet come."** *⁵ His mother said to the servants, "Do whatever he tells you."*

I appreciate the Amplified Bible's rendering of verses two and three. It more accurately portrays the issue we are discussing:

³ And when the wine was all gone, the mother of Jesus said to Him, They have no more wine! **⁴ Jesus said to her, [Dear] woman, what is that to you and to Me? [What do we have in common? Leave it to Me.] My time (hour to act) has not yet come.**

Mary did not know the true identity of Jesus. That is, she did not know what Gabriel meant when he said Jesus would be "the Son of the Most High." But she knew He was special. She knew He was chosen by God for greatness. So when she heard that there was no more wine, she expectantly turned to her son and basically said, "*Now* is the time. Act, my son. Vindicate your name *and mine.*"

Jesus loved Mary as both His mother and His child. He *would* vindicate her name and His. But He also knew this request wasn't only about glorifying His name. It was about removing her shame and embarrassment. He knew that what Mary was essentially asking Him was, "Sic 'em, Jesus." Jesus asked her a simple question: "What does this miracle have to do with our relationship and what others think about us? The time for My vindication from God (and yours) has not yet come."

Mary seemed to understand. Jesus *did* act, and He continued to act and glorify His Father. Yet He made it clear it wasn't about Him—or her. There were flashes of deity in His indignation at the slanderous insults hurled at Him. He warned that the Son of Man would also be the future Judge of all who so casually mocked Him (Matthew 12:36-37; 16:27), but for the most part, He held His peace. There would be a time when every knee would bow and every tongue would acknowledge who He really was (Philippians 2:10). Nevertheless, many would still reject Him and slander Him while He was on earth, just like they would slander Mary and reject what she knew to be true for the rest of her earthly life.

2 Corinthians 6:2 (RSV)
... "**At the acceptable time** I have listened to you, and helped you on the day of salvation."...

Just like Jesus' ultimate vindication, Mary's "acceptable time" has still not come. Your life may be similar to Mary's. There may be some wrong that needs to be righted. There may be some weight that you are living under that, while God has given you some relief, your vindication and victory has not yet fully arrived. From God's perspective, it is not the acceptable time for your ultimate deliverance. Like Mary's life, you may not be told *why* it isn't the acceptable time, or *when* the acceptable time may come in this earthly life.

There is no formulaic answer for when you will be delivered or even why not. In retrospect, we can see God's timing in waiting to glorify Jesus as the obvious and apparent King of all the earth. Yet with our lives, it can be difficult to see any clear reason why the time is not right.

2 Samuel 22:31
*This God—**his way is perfect**; the word of the L*ORD *proves true; he is a shield for all those who take refuge in him.*

Psalm 37:5-6 (RSV)
*Commit your way to the L*ORD*; trust in him, and he will act. [6] **He will bring forth your vindication as the light, and your right as the noonday.***

We have seen so many negative examples of those who would not wait on God's timing for their wishes and desires. Wait for God's timing in your deliverance. It is always perfect.

11 ABRAHAM—GOD SETTING THE STAGE

Genesis 13:14-17

¹⁴ *The* LORD *said to Abram, after Lot had separated from him, "Lift up your eyes and look from the place where you are, northward and southward and eastward and westward,* ¹⁵ ***for all the land that you see I will give to you and to your offspring forever.*** ¹⁶ *I will make your offspring as the dust of the earth, so that if one can count the dust of the earth, your offspring also can be counted.* ¹⁷ *Arise, walk through the length and the breadth of the land,* ***for I will give it to you.****"*

A promise was made to Abraham (he was Abram at the time, but for the sake of clarity, let's refer to him as Abraham). It was a very specific promise. God told Abraham, as he walked through the length and breadth of Canaan, that all the land he saw would be his. But while God proved faithful to make him rich and respected in the land, Abraham had no heir and he possessed no land. Abraham was later told that God would indeed give him an heir. But he was also told that he would not possess the land in his mortal life. The promise would be fulfilled, but there would be a "detour" as far as Abraham's perspective was concerned.

Genesis 15:13-16

*13 Then the LORD said to Abram, "Know for certain that your offspring will be sojourners in a land that is not theirs and will be servants there, and they will be afflicted for four hundred years. 14 But I will bring judgment on the nation that they serve, and afterward they shall come out with great possessions. 15 As for you, you shall go to your fathers in peace; you shall be buried in a good old age. 16 And they shall come back here in the fourth generation, **for the iniquity of the Amorites is not yet complete.**"*

Abraham was given an explanation of his detour most of us do not get:

- His descendants would not immediately live in this Promised Land. It wouldn't occur for another 400 years.

- God would deliver his descendants. They would not only be freed from the people who oppressed them, but they would also plunder their oppressors and acquire great wealth.
- Acquiring possession of the Promised Land would take this long because, in God's timing, His judgment of the people who inhabited the land was not ready to be executed.

I wonder how much Abraham really understood about that conversation. "Live to a good old age, go to my fathers in peace. That sounds good. My offspring will be afflicted for 400 years and come out with great possessions. But part of the "why" all this will take so long is that a nation is not yet ready to be judged? It seems simple, but maybe not as simple as I thought."

It *wasn't as simple as he thought.* Abraham believed the promise. After that conversation with the Lord, one thing was clear: he wouldn't possess this land in his lifetime. He would possess it later. But when? When you look back at the promise in Genesis 13:14-17, the promise Abraham received wasn't just "delayed" because of events that would happen in Egypt and Canaan 400 years into the future. It was likely delayed (depending on your end time views) because the promise referred to an event that would not be fulfilled until at least *4000 plus years had passed.* That event would be called the Millennium. Abraham would have had no idea his promise from God would generate heated debates regarding whether the promise was, in fact, describing Israel's borders in the Millennium or the Promised Land of the Eternal Future. Even though that promise initially looked and sounded fairly straightforward to Abraham, it's fair to say the promise was, indeed, *very complicated.*

Abraham's promise is similar to Mary's. Both promises were delayed from their perspectives. Both promises required waiting on God's timing. Mary was simply told that it wasn't the acceptable time. Abraham was told *why* it wasn't the acceptable time.

The explanation God gave Abraham gives us a different insight into why promises are "delayed." God is invisibly setting the stage of our future. Some of the details of Abraham's promise had direct implications for his life. Other details of his promise had little to do with his time on earth. The outcome of these future events all depended on the seemingly insignificant choices Abraham made in his life.

There may be promises you are sure God has given you that are not being fulfilled. In fact, it may seem that if anything, based on your present circumstances, the possibility of those promises ever being fulfilled in your lifetime looks dim. But just like Abraham's promise, it may be much more complicated than you think. God is setting the stage for events in the future. There are unrelated people and events being interwoven over time that are completely invisible to you now. Like Abraham, some of those events and people will eventually have direct influence in your life; some may never affect your life on this earth.

Yet, unknown to you, God has made *you* the focal point of the changes He is creating, just like Abraham was the focal point of many future actions. God is actively working regarding those promises He gave you about the future. He doesn't ask for—nor does He need—your help in this incredible task. He just asks you to trust Him as He sets the stage.

12 PETER—NOT MATURE ENOUGH

John 13:36-38

*36 Simon Peter said to him, "Lord, where are you going?" Jesus answered him, "Where I am going you cannot follow me now, but you will follow afterward." 37 Peter said to him, "Lord, why can I not follow you now? I will lay down my life for you." 38 Jesus answered, "**Will you lay down your life for me?** Truly, truly, I say to you, the rooster will not crow till you have denied me three times.*

Peter meant what he said. I don't think Peter was boastfully talking off the top of his head in the passage above, either to impress his Lord or the other disciples. He heard someone was going to betray the Lord. He likely understood that meant there was going to be a fight, hence the disciples asking Jesus about swords (Luke 22:38). Peter proved he was willing to fight—though he also proved he wasn't a particularly good fighter—by lashing out and cutting off the ear (opposed to the head) of the servant of the high priest (Matthew 25:51).

But when Jesus told Peter to stop and healed the "enemy" he was trying to kill, something began to happen within him. When Jesus merely rebuked His attackers and then meekly submitted to them as they bound Him in chains, Peter's resolve weakened. Peter was ready for a fight, but not this type of fight. It seemed like surrender to him. Surely there was an inward cry in his heart of, "Every man for himself!" For it seemed the cause—the Man—whom he was willing to die for, simply evaporated before his eyes.

Of course, that wasn't true. Jesus had told the disciples several times that He was to be arrested, beaten, and killed when they made their final trip to Jerusalem (Matthew 20:18; Luke 9:44, for example). However, Peter envisioned this event differently. It's not that he didn't understand this promise because it was open-ended like Mary's. Nor was it because it was more complex than it had initially looked, as Abraham's promise was. Peter didn't understand the promise because he wasn't *ready* to understand. He wasn't spiritually mature enough to grasp what Jesus said, let alone what He was doing.

Peter *would* die for his Lord, but much had to change within him before then. God would use him greatly during the course of his life, but Peter first needed to mature. The same is true for you and me regarding some of the promises or spiritual ambitions He has given us.

And that can be extremely frustrating, can't it? For you can't make your "maturing journey" go any faster than the speed at which it is supposed to go, any more so than I can make my garden bear vegetables as fast as I would like. I can fertilize, water, and weed my garden more frequently. While that will help the overall health and vigor of the plants, it won't typically cause the plants to bring their fruit to maturity any quicker. The maturation time for each individual vegetable has already been more or less established, regardless of how much I try and push it along.

Unfortunately, there are too many examples of young athletes and actors who were not mature enough to handle the fame and fortune that were thrust on them. The same is true for managers who were promoted too soon and young couples who married when they should have waited. Many times, the things we want so badly would actually turn out to be a curse if they were granted to us when we wanted them *because we were not mature enough yet.*

As I look back over my life, I realize that I was not mature enough—both as a man and a Christian—for the things I thought God should have granted to me at the time I wanted them. I'm also sure there are things that God has promised me that have not been granted because He knows I'm *still* not spiritually mature enough for those things. Just like me, maybe God has given you a promise and it's not happening yet. It doesn't necessarily mean there is blatant or hidden sin in your life. It doesn't even mean there may be glaring weaknesses in your Christian walk or ministry.

It may simply mean that, as far as God is concerned, you're not ready to handle what you think He has promised. There are other lessons to learn—through people and events that are not even on the visible horizon of your life—that you have to experience in order for you to grow. These are lessons that you cannot force and you cannot manufacture. They will happen where and when God determines that they should.

In some ways, that reason to wait on a promise from God is much more difficult than the others we have discussed. It's difficult because it doesn't involve waiting for God to set up something or someone else in the future. Nor is it about simply waiting a given number of years before something happens. It's difficult because it involves waiting for God to set up and change *you.* While sanctification involves both God's and our efforts, the fact is, you and I can't rush this process. Unlike my garden, there is no set time frame in this process.

That's what makes it so frustrating; since the promise hinges on *our* maturity, we feel we are in control of our promise because we believe we can easily change ourselves. The problem is that we're really not in control at all. Having lengthy quiet times and memorizing Scripture will broaden my knowledge of Christ, but it won't necessarily speed up the process of me *becoming like Christ.* These activities are certainly better for my spiritual health than not doing them at all. But, it's not going to force God's hand in forming me into the person He wants me to be just because I want Him to act sooner rather than later.

It's also frustrating because becoming Christlike is precisely what God wants in my life (Ephesians 4:13). So the intuitive thing to think is that God would want to bring that about—if I am willing—just as quickly as He could. God isn't bound by time, so He brings about events according to His perfect timing, and that includes my maturity in Christ.

In my vegetable garden, maturity is a relatively slow process. Thankfully, it is noticeable, but just noticeable. Like Peter, we need to learn that God's maturing process in our spiritual lives also takes time—a lifetime.

DISAPPOINTMENT AND ETERNAL PERSPECTIVES

Our last six character studies have to do with choices and detours in our lives. They also deal with eternal perspectives related to those two issues.

We all make scores of choices each day, from the trivial (what soda I choose) to the critical (what career I pick). All of these choices have baseline assumptions (regardless of what soda I choose, it should be safe to drink) and assumptive questions (What career will benefit me more?).

Sometimes our assumptions and assumptive questions are wrong, because our eternal perspectives are wrong. What do I mean by an "eternal perspective?" For the purpose of this study, let's simply define that as thinking the way

God thinks about things. It involves how God wants to accomplish His goals on earth and how He wants men and women to conform to those goals. We will examine three people—three *righteous* people—who had the wrong assumptions about what or how God's goals and plans were to be accomplished through them.

The companion issue—from a strictly human perspective—is how we view detours in our lives. Even when we believe we have God's perspective or, at least, when we are living in obedience to Him in the path He has given us, life can feel like one big detour.

Of course, it's not a detour at all. Many times life feels "detoured" because our perspectives are focused on the short term. We think if God would just hurry up and get us through the detour, our life could begin again, and we would be able to accomplish His goals and plans.

What we will see from three other people— whom the Bible also described as righteous—is that there was nothing temporary about their detour. The "detour" *was* His plan for their life, their *entire* life.

We will begin with Joshua and choosing sides.

13 JOSHUA—CHOOSING SIDES

Joshua 5:13-14

*13 When Joshua was by Jericho, he lifted up his eyes and looked, and behold, a man was standing before him with his drawn sword in his hand. And Joshua went to him and said to him, "**Are you for us, or for our adversaries?**" 14 And he said, "**No; but I am the commander of the army of the L*ord*.** Now I have come." And Joshua fell on his face to the earth and worshiped and said to him, "What does my lord say to his servant?"*

Joshua met a Man on the plain of Jericho. He did not know that Man was the Pre-Incarnate Christ, but after he spoke with Him, he must have known he was speaking with God. Joshua asked the Lord a straightforward question: are you on our side or on our enemies' side? God's answer was equally blunt and to the point. What God essentially told Joshua was, "I'm not on your side or your enemies' side. *I'm on My side.*"

I'm sure that statement was puzzling to Joshua. There is nothing in the narrative that implied that Joshua needed to be rebuked for his presumptuous behavior. After all, God had promised that He would be Israel's Protector and Shield (Deuteronomy 33:29). In fact, just a few days earlier, God had promised Joshua that He would be with him and not forsake him (Joshua 1:5). But apparently, God needed to clarify a point for Joshua. Yes, He would be the source of their strength and deliverance, but the battles He would fight for Israel were ultimately for *His* glory, not theirs. The goals and objectives Israel had been given would be accomplished according to *His* will, not theirs.

This statement from the Lord was an attitude adjustment for Joshua. Joshua, as Israel's commander, saw the Commander of the army of the Lord and asked if He was on his side—implying *under* Joshua's authority and direction. Jesus told Joshua that *He* was the One in control, and the unspoken question from Him was, "*Are you on My side?*"

God answering our questions of His commitment to us with *His* pointed questions regarding our character can be hard to accept. God is supposed to be *for me* as a Christian (Romans 8:31). Why the equivocation from God on this point in the Book of Joshua? It seems His answer to Joshua should have been a definite, "Yes, I am for you! Go, conquer the land!" But as I said, something needed to be clarified for Joshua, just like it needs to be made clear to us. God is good to me because it glorifies Him. God is for me because it honors Him. God grants my prayer requests and secret desires because it shows Him—first and foremost—as the Glorious Father.

There may be times you have asked or are even asking right now, "As Your child, *are* You for me, Lord?" The answer from the Lord is, "Yes, because I'm for Me first. Everything I desire is for My glory, which is *good for you*, for all of mankind, and for all of Creation. If I were simply "for you," then all you would have is an all-powerful Guru, Genie, and Personal Bodyguard who is at your beckon call. However, the problem with that idea is your desires and plans are not perfect."

"So if I granted your desires and plans just as you wanted, the results—as you have seen through the lives of others in the Bible—might not turn out the way you'd like. Worse, they might be destructive for generations to come. As C.S. Lewis wrote of Me in *The Chronicles of Narnia*, I'm not a tame Lion. You can't put Me on a leash to do your will, any more so than Joshua could on the plain of Jericho, and that's a *good thing*. You need to align your plans with Mine, not the other way around."

Luke 6:38
*"For I have come down from heaven, **not to do my own will** but the will of him who sent me."*

This quote from Jesus is what we discussed in *When God Disappoints.* It's not just the beginning of assessing God's will for us regarding a specific issue in our life that may be disappointing us. It is actually the first step in evaluating how we look at our *entire* life's mission. As we saw with Jonah, we can honestly believe we want to follow God's will for our life, but we typically also want to do it *our way.* We are convinced we are on His side, but many times, *we are really on our side.* Our motivation is ultimately about "what's in it for me?"

Just like Joshua, before you begin the battle—whether that battle is a journey you didn't expect regarding employment, relationships, health or whatever you're facing—this issue needs to be resolved in your life. It doesn't mean it will permanently be settled this side of heaven. It will involve a lifetime of separate decisions on these types of issues. But the starting question on the resolution of anything in your life begins with this question: *"Are you on My side?"*

14 SAMUEL—WHEN "GOOD" IS BAD

1 Samuel 16:1; 6-7

*The L*ORD *said to Samuel, "How long will you grieve over Saul, since I have rejected him from being king over Israel? Fill your horn with oil, and go. I will send you to Jesse the Bethlehemite, for I have provided for myself a king among his sons."*
*⁶ When they came, [Samuel] looked on Eliab [one of Jesse's sons] and thought, "Surely the L*ORD*'s anointed is before him." ⁷ But the L*ORD *said to Samuel, "**Do not look on his appearance or on the height of his stature**, because I have rejected him. For the L*ORD *sees not as man sees: man looks on the outward appearance, but the L*ORD *looks on the heart."*

We are continually faced with the challenge of determining the appearance of "good" versus what truly is good. As we have seen, things that look like good choices to us can be horribly bad choices in the long run. Conversely, things that seem like bad circumstances, even hopeless circumstances, can prove to be the best possible thing that could have happened to us. Samuel was faced with this same dilemma.

Like Joshua, Samuel was a righteous man who was walking closely with the Lord. It's not that his presumption of who the Lord might want as king over Israel in 1 Samuel 16 was silly or sinful. In fact, just the opposite; for when Saul was chosen by God, Samuel saw that he was "...*a handsome young man. There was not a man among the people of Israel more handsome than he. **From his shoulders upward he was taller than any of the people*** (1 Samuel 9:2).

God chose Saul—from Samuel's perspective—based on how good a "fit" he would be for the need at hand. In that case, the "need at hand" was a warrior/leader of Israel. He was handsome (attractive people are more accepted and admired as leaders). He was also taller and, likely, bigger than the men of Israel (physically imposing men inspire confidence and gain submission more readily as leaders). Eliab seemed to be this kind of man.

God told Samuel "no." The schematic in Samuel's mind that he assumed to be God's will was all wrong. God told Samuel that Eliab's heart was not with Him. If you read further into 1 Samuel 16, you will see Samuel didn't debate this decision with God. He already knew what it was like to have a man in a position of power not be truly faithful to God, and the results were disastrous. While the narrative does not say this, it is likely Samuel nodded in understanding when the Lord told him that men make decisions based on appearances. When he remembered Saul, he knew the condition of a man's heart toward God was the most important parameter in evaluating a man's worth.

We make the same mistakes, too, only our decisions don't involve choosing kings. The decision may involve choosing someone who is handsome/beautiful, smart, and charming as our spouse. It may involve some job that features lucrative pay and attractive perks. It may involve a choice that will take us down a path that we believe will lead to a more comfortable, carefree life. What can be frustrating about all this is, like Samuel, we may be in close communion with the Lord. We may be evaluating matters sensibly and logically based on our present circumstances and the apparent options that are given to us. Yet, we can choose just as incorrectly as Samuel.

Unlike Samuel, however, most of us are not audibly told by God not to choose a person, position, or path that seems perfectly reasonable. How can we know if our decision is truly good or bad? Many times, God uses a two-step process in this revelation. The first step is that God "speaks" to us through circumstances; our prayer requests and "good" desires *are not granted.*

Christians can fall into the snare of disappointment and bitterness when they keep seeking some "good" thing they desire, yet God either hinders that pursuit or outright prevents it from happening. The reason He may be doing this—just like He did with Samuel—is the something we seek that seems so sensible, logical, and helpful in our life is really poison. Just as Eliab would have been another Saul for Israel (and another heartbreak for Samuel), God knows some of the "good" things we seek would be that way for us, too. Therefore, He says "no" through circumstances. He takes away what we think is "good" for our lives.

That taking away usually leads us to the second step: personal introspection. After figuratively banging our heads against the wall, wondering why what seems such an obviously good thing is not being granted by the Lord, questions usually begin to come to mind. Questions such as these:

- *Why* do I want this so badly?
- Is there really something else driving my desire?
- If God doesn't want me to have this, what would *He* think isn't good about it?
- Am I really content in the circumstances of my life, or do I feel I need to be "somewhere" else?

I know it's a silly example, but in the animated movie *Kung Fu Panda* (DreamWorks, 2008), Po is rigorously trained in Kung Fu by being denied the thing he loved most—food. In and of itself, food is not a bad thing. Yet by the end of his training, he realized food was not that important to him anymore. There were bigger and grander things that he now cared about. God speaks to us the same way concerning the "good" things we think we need in our lives. He denies what we think we want and shows us what really is important to Him.

15 ANANIAS—WHEN "BAD" IS GOOD

Acts 9:10-16

[10] *Now there was a disciple at Damascus named Ananias. The Lord said to him in a vision, "Ananias." And he said, "Here I am, Lord."* [11] *And the Lord said to him, "Rise and go to the street called Straight, and at the house of Judas look for a man of Tarsus named Saul, for behold, he is praying,* [12] *and he has seen in a vision a man named Ananias come in and lay his hands on him so that he might regain his sight."* [13] *But Ananias answered,* **"Lord, I have heard from many about this man, how much evil he has done to your saints at Jerusalem.** [14] *And here he has authority from the chief priests to bind all who call on your name."* [15] **But the Lord said to him, "Go, for he is a chosen instrument of mine to carry my name**

before the Gentiles and kings and the children of Israel. [16] *For I will show him how much he must suffer for the sake of my name."*

We don't know much about Ananias. He was a devout man (Acts 22:12). He very likely was a leader in the Church at Damascus. From the passage above, we also know that he knew about Saul. In fact, many had testified to him that Saul was "bad news" as far Christians were concerned. Many were frightened of Saul in Damascus, Ananias included. It wouldn't surprise me at all that many of those Christians had a similar attitude towards Saul that Jonah had towards Nineveh— "Lord, take out Saul."

Being told to welcome Saul into his house and heal him probably hit Ananias like a bucket of cold water in the face. "No, Lord, I don't think You understand. Saul is the enemy. *Your* enemy, not just mine. The only "good" news I heard in Your announcement was that he was blind. Don't You think it best—for the *good of Your Church*—that he stay that way?"

No, actually, God didn't. The Lord had big plans for Saul. God wouldn't just change his name and his character. He would change Saul's mission in life, and in doing so, He would set in motion the evangelization of the Roman Empire.

We can't blame Ananias for his thought process. It had to be puzzling to Ananias to be commanded to reach out and help Saul. In spite of the Lord Jesus' commandment to love our enemies and pray for those who persecute us (Matthew 5:44), there is something counter-intuitive about helping someone evil. Even worse, it would feel *traitorous* to help someone who is actively persecuting God's people.

That's the other side of the appearance of "good" and "bad": sometimes "bad" things really are good. I referenced Matthew 5:44, but really most of Matthew chapter five seems counter-intuitive, doesn't it? Apart from suffering for Jesus' sake, what "good" comes from turning the other cheek to someone who hit me in the first place? What "good" is accomplished by giving someone my cloak if they steal my shirt? What "good" occurs at all by not resisting someone who is evil?

Of course, there are many stories of great good that have occurred with those who followed Jesus' words. Like Paul, people came to Christ, families and communities were changed, even whole generations and nations were changed because of something that seemed "bad" that God transformed into good.

Unfortunately, you and I routinely have Ananias' reaction to being gracious or merciful to someone evil. And maybe not just to *someone*, but to *something* evil that has happened in our lives, whether that involves our health, job, or personal relationships.

A Christian friend recently told me something like this: "I notice when things are not going as well or as easy as I would like, I pray more and things generally turn out well. When things are easy, neat and tidy, I become complacent about prayer and things generally turn out worse than I would like."

That's just one of the outcomes we discussed at the beginning of this book when we talked about the storms God sends our way. When "bad" comes in our lives, we pray more (which is good). We have to depend on and trust God more regarding what is happening in our lives (which is also good).

That said, it doesn't mean the evil that comes into our lives isn't really evil or that the pain and sadness it causes is somehow just an illusion. When the Lord Jesus was crucified, the scourging He received was excruciatingly painful. His ordeal on the cross was equally torturous. The Father hurling innumerable eternal sentences of hell on Him literally broke His heart. But the evil He endured was for a greater good. In fact, it accomplished the greatest blessing of God for this sinful world.

That's true for you and me as well. Evil *will* come into our lives. "Bad" things will loom on the horizon. Sometimes evil circumstances seem to strand us, as if we were on some desert island and we feel we cannot escape. Sometimes evil circumstances seem to reshape the direction of our life. Our goals are the same, but the "how," "when," and "where" of what is happening is not in sync with what we think should be happening.

The eternal perspective lesson for us in Ananias' story (and similar stories in the Bible) is evil coming into our lives will not destroy our lives. It does not have to be the dominate fixture of our lives. God—to the great consternation of Satan— *uses evil for good*. We typically regard all of these things as "detours" in our lives—evil that seemingly has redirected our life in a bad way. We will see from the next three individuals in the Bible that the key word in this discussion is "seemingly," for great good came out of these detours.

16 JOSEPH—THE UNSEEN MISSION

Genesis 50:19-20

¹⁹ But Joseph said to them, "Do not fear, for am I in the place of God? ²⁰ **As for you, you meant evil against me, but God meant it for good,** to bring it about that many people should be kept alive, as they are today.

We have already discussed Joseph in chapter two, but that was regarding God's refining storms in his life. We need to look at Joseph's life in a different way—the way *he* might have viewed how and what would be the direction of his life. Joseph was seventeen when he had those prophetic dreams from God. He was living his life as a nomadic shepherd and, likely, he thought the remainder of his life would be spent in this pursuit.

What about those dreams? All he knew was that God said he would rule over his brothers (unlikely as the second youngest) and over his mother and father (disrespectfully impertinent, hence the rebuke from Jacob in Genesis 37:10).

What would those dreams look like when they were fulfilled? Hard to say. Maybe he would be blessed like his great grandfather Abraham and acquire more possessions and people than his brothers or his father. Maybe it was just a symbolic dream that meant Joseph would be wiser than the rest of his family. Joseph knew the dream was from God, and it would be fulfilled. Other than that, the "how," "what," "where," and especially, "when" were completely unknown. That doesn't mean Joseph didn't try and ponder this mystery and experiment with different scenarios in his mind.

One scenario I'm sure he *didn't* expect was to be kidnapped by his brothers and sold into slavery. One scenario wasn't that he would be eventually made the manager of a rich Egyptian's household, only to be later thrown into prison for *not* taking advantage of the master's wife. It's very easy to suppose that Joseph thought his life had taken a wild detour away from the dreams he had been given from God. As he sat in that dark, musty dungeon, it would have been very easy for him to think that the dream God had given him wasn't about life on earth at all. Maybe it was a picture of his reward in Heaven, for it would seem to him that God's promise—like Abraham's promise for an heir when he was very old—had little shot of being accomplished on this earth.

The dream was fulfilled—literally—when his brothers bowed before him seeking grain, and when his father acknowledged his son's power in the land of Egypt. However, as we know from the passage quoted at the beginning of this chapter, the dream involved much more than that. It was about saving Israel (the man and the nation) from oblivion, due to the famine that had struck the eastern Mediterranean. It was about incubating Jacob's family in a wealthy and secure land so that they could prosper and multiply into a great nation. It was also about placing Israel in the hands of a nation that would eventually oppress them until the time of their deliverance from God. All of this would be accomplished by the "detour" that was Joseph's life.

Joseph had no idea about any of this. For much of Joseph's life, what unfolded before him was worse than Mr. Toad's Wild Ride. It was a nightmare. Why couldn't God have specifically told

Joseph more of what was going to transpire in his life? Imagine this scenario for a moment. You are seventeen and God comes to you in a dream one night. He quietly sits next to you and explains your future. "My child," He says, "My plan for your life is for you to be taken away from your home. You will be sold as a slave by your siblings, learn management and delegation in your position as a slave, and then be thrust into prison for obeying My commandments. You will eventually be brought to a position of power and you will save your family from extinction."

"But you will never see your home again—not in this life. You will not see your father again until he is old and frail. And you will need to forgive your siblings and not be vindictive to them, for they will need to grow and prosper their families in this foreign land."

"I will be with you. But look around and remember as best you can, as your great grandfather Abraham did. For as I said, *you will never see your homeland again*."

Be honest with yourself: would you voluntarily go through with God's plan? Or would you try as hard as you could—like Moses did with the mission God gave him—to talk God out of this scenario? Most of us would do the latter. There is a reason

God does not reveal the course of our lives in precise detail. Given the choice, we would not want to follow through with most of it—even knowing there would be a happy ending. So He gives us a promise from His Word to hold on to or a dream to cling to when life seems to be veering in a direction it's not supposed to be going, *without giving us all the details.*

Joseph's detour wasn't really a detour at all. It was God's original plan. Many of our "detours" in life are like Joseph's. We can either become bitter or resentful that things didn't go the way we scripted them in our minds, or we can trust God through the detour and, in faith, believe that a bigger plan, a grander mission, is in store for us.

17 LEAH—THE FORSAKEN MARRIAGE

Genesis 29:31; 30:14-15

"When the LORD saw that **Leah was hated**, he opened her womb, but Rachel was barren."

14 In the days of wheat harvest Reuben went and found mandrakes in the field and brought them to his mother Leah. Then Rachel said to Leah, "Please give me some of your son's mandrakes." 15 But she said to her, "Is it a small matter that you have taken away my husband? Would you take away my son's mandrakes also?"

Leah was not delusional when she told Rachel that Rachel had taken away *her* husband. I know Jacob was never in love with Leah—he wanted her sister. I also know it wasn't Rachel's fault that her father played a cruel trick on her sister and drug her into Jacob's and Rachel's relationship. But the fact is—before God—Leah was Jacob's legitimate first wife. Jacob and Rachel could have said marriage vows till midnight, but *the marriage ceremony was first consummated between Jacob and Leah.* Leah may have been perceived by Jacob and Rachel as the interloper in their marriage (actually, it was Laban). But as far as God was concerned, *Rachel* was the second wife, not Leah.

That didn't matter to Jacob. He always wanted Rachel, and he knew he had been tricked. He also knew Leah was his wife, so he couldn't divorce her. Therefore, he simply ignored her. Leah thought sons would please Jacob, just as they would have pleased any husband in that era. It didn't matter. Six sons didn't matter to Jacob. She was still ignored. It saddens me when I think of Genesis 30:14-16, and realize Leah basically had to bribe Rachel just so she could be intimate with her husband—just to feel wanted, to be touched and caressed—since it seems it happened so rarely.

Leah didn't want this detour in her life. Nowhere in Scripture does it state (or even imply) that Leah secretly loved Jacob while he was serving Laban for the right to marry Rachel. What she wanted was a husband who would love and take care of her in an exclusive, intimate relationship. What she wanted was to build a family without all the drama of another woman vying for—and winning—her husband's attention and affection.

Most of the people we have examined had a life with a happy ending. Leah's life does not. Scripture does not record Jacob having a change of heart towards Leah. In fact, as we have already discussed in chapter eight, Jacob doted over Joseph and Benjamin—Rachel's sons—and ignored Leah's. Rachel's death brings Jacob sorrow (Genesis 48:7). Leah's epitaph is a simple footnote from him: "… *in the cave that is in the field at Machpelah, to the east of Mamre, in the land of Canaan…there I buried Leah…"* (Genesis 49:30-31).

Scripture also does not record God giving Leah any promise of hope or comfort through her life, as He did with Sarah and Rebekah. Even Hagar—one of Abraham's *concubines*—received a promise from God (Genesis 21:17-18). Leah suffered in silence. Nor was she permitted to know the outcome of any of her sons. In fact, when she knew them, they were likely bitter and resentful of the way their father treated their mother. Yet Scripture says God took notice of her and pitied her. That also implies, as God did with Joseph, that He was actively caring for her and protecting her.

I cannot help but think there are many Christian Leahs throughout the world. They silently suffer in marriages that are going nowhere. They are raising children to fear the Lord—as best they can—with little help from pre-occupied husbands. They yearn to have a husband love them and care for them as God commanded husbands to do (Ephesians 5:25), but like Leah, they are simply role players in their home. This is not a short detour in these women's lives. *Their whole life seems like a huge, tragic detour.*

Maybe you are one of them. Like Leah, God may be silent in your suffering. And sadly, my dear sister, on this earth, your life may not have a happy ending either. But there may be things that God is doing through you and through your children that are so far over the horizon that you or anyone else cannot see right now—just like it was for Leah.

Leah had six sons. Two of them you should note: Levi and Judah. Without Leah, there is no Levi. That means *there is no Moses.* Without Leah, there is no Judah. That means *there is no David, no Solomon, no Christ.* The relevance of Leah's life was enormous, yet she, nor anyone else, would know it for hundreds of years.

I did not quote the entirety of Genesis 49 regarding Leah. While Jacob mentions her in terse brevity, the fact is—likely inadvertently—he praises her by describing how he is to be buried:

Genesis 49:29-32

*29 Then he [Jacob] commanded them and said to them, "I am to be gathered to my people; **bury me with my fathers in the cave that is in the field of Ephron the Hittite,** 30 in the cave that is in the field at Machpelah, to the east of Mamre, in the land of Canaan, which Abraham bought with the field from Ephron the Hittite to possess as a burying place. 31 **There they buried Abraham and Sarah** his wife. There they buried **Isaac and Rebekah** his wife, **and there I buried Leah**— 32 the field and the cave that is in it were bought from the Hittites."*

The memorial patriarchal tomb contained Abraham and Sarah, Isaac and Rebekah. It also contained Jacob and *Leah*—not Rachel—Jacob's true and long-suffering wife. Leah, the mother of Levi, ancestral mother to the priests of God. Leah, the mother of Judah, ancestral mother to the True and Eternal King of Israel. Like many who would come after her, Leah's life had great significance in her seemingly insignificant detour.

18 PAUL—THE LONG WAY AROUND

Romans 15:23-25

*23 But now, since I no longer have any room for work in these regions, and since I have longed for many years to come to you, 24 **I hope to see you in passing as I go to Spain, and to be helped on my journey there by you, once I have enjoyed your company for a while.** 25 At present, **however, I am going to Jerusalem bringing aid to the saints**.*

Whether Paul made it to Spain or not, we do not know. It's clear he believed he was going to Jerusalem to deliver the offerings he had collected and then head out again on his fourth missionary journey to Rome and Spain. In his mind, the work that he needed to accomplish in the eastern

Mediterranean was done. It was time to move on to the western Mediterranean. God obviously wanted Paul in Rome, as well. But He had a different plan for eventually getting him there.

Paul was warned in Acts 21:10-12 that he would be bound and imprisoned at the hands of the Jews in Jerusalem, so he knew this was coming. Though Paul said in that passage that he was willing to die in Jerusalem, I don't believe he could have imagined the scenario that unfolded:

- The Romans would actually *help* him escape from Jerusalem.
- He would spend at least two years in prison in Caesarea and eventually appeal to Caesar.
- He would be lost at sea, shipwrecked on the island of Malta, and finally arrive in Rome—in chains and under house arrest.

Paul's original desire to minister to the Church in Rome was what God wanted to happen. But *how* and *when* that came about—in spite of the warning he had received in Ephesus—was probably surprising to him. That doesn't mean he was frustrated or disappointed in God. On the contrary, Paul showed by his words and actions that he was quite content to be led wherever God wanted him to go. Paul said he was ready to be martyred in Jerusalem at the hands of the Jews. The irony is that the Romans who helped him escape certain martyrdom at the hands of the Jews would be the ones who would execute him, just as they had executed his Lord.

The eternal perspective lesson from Paul's ministry is that God oftentimes plants a desire or goal in our heart to move in some direction. Whether it involves ministry, a secular job, or a relationship, He causes us to act on these desires—with the knowledge we have at the moment—and moves us forward. Being human, we plot our steps for the future and imagine outcomes. However, the outcomes that we are so sure will follow our well-made plans often don't occur. Unlike Paul, what usually happens in our hearts is we get puzzled and frustrated by what appear to be setbacks or outright failure.

If God is the One who put those desires in our hearts, then He will bring the outcomes. However, as we have seen from other people in the Bible, it usually doesn't occur the way we expect, let alone when we expect it.

In summary, we examined six people regarding eternal perspectives and disappointment with God.

We learned that:

- Before we begin to assess what God will or won't do in our life, we need to determine whether our heart is truly on His side or our side.
- Things that initially look good aren't always good. In fact, they can have long-term, disastrous consequences.
- Things that initially look bad aren't as crushingly destructive as we might think. God is not thwarted by evil, therefore His ultimate plans for our lives aren't either.
- God deliberately gives promises to us in a cryptic way, because He knows we cannot handle the details regarding the path of our life. His plans for us are also multi-faceted. They simultaneously change us in the image of His Son and they affect change in people, society, and the world.
- God doesn't always allow us to have storybook, happy endings—as far as our life is concerned. However, what can appear insignificant over the course of an entire life can be enormously significant in the generations that follow.

- God very often grants the desires of our hearts, but those desires typically are not fulfilled how or when we expect it.

FINAL THOUGHTS

It would be impossible for me to summarize all these lessons in a few bullet points. Further, the point of these studies is to have you try and relate to an individual or individuals regarding your own specific struggles with God. However, if I were to sit down with one of my sons or a close friend who was struggling with disappointment in God, and I only had five minutes to try and impart some wisdom on this subject, there are three things I would emphasize.

Take the sword out of your hands

Most of the chaos and heartache we observed in the individuals we studied was due to their own impatience with God. Specifically, that impatience grew out of their unfulfilled desire to have God vindicate them, restore them, or punish those who had wronged them. When we try and "deliver" ourselves—either by forcing open the closed doors of our lives or punishing others for wrongs they have committed against us—we usually botch things up.

That doesn't mean that if the opportunity to fulfill a desire or dream in your life arises, you shouldn't jump at it. It doesn't mean that you shouldn't confront and rebuke evil (either personal or corporate) that comes into your life. But way too often, we do this according to our sinful impulses and our carnal nature. We generally don't do these things with a Spirit-led, self-controlled, self-denying attitude.

There is a reason God said, "*Vengeance is Mine; I will repay*" (Romans 12:19; Deuteronomy 32:35). We can also confidently say that it is only God who delivers and brings blessings, who lifts up one and sets down another (Psalm 75:6-7). Only God can accomplish this by perfectly interweaving judgment and blessing, restoring and requiting.

Quit trying to "figure out" what God is doing

When I was visiting a break room in a business office one day, I noticed a sign that gave a list of performance evaluations for their management team. One of those points was, "Performs effectively in an ambiguous and complex environment." You might not care to have that as one of the criteria that measures the performance for *your job*, but as far as your *Christian life* is concerned—regarding understanding how God deals with you—it's not a bad place to start.

God's plans often *seem* ambiguous. Even when you feel assured about a desire, dream or direction you believe God has implanted in you, trying to discern the *specific* direction you are moving in is not always easy. In fact, that specific direction can seem worse than ambiguous. At times, the direction you feel you are going can seem puzzling and pointless. That is because God's plans are also *complex*. Many translations of Romans 11:33 describe God's ways as "unsearchable," "inscrutable," "unfathomable."

God's plans are interwoven seamlessly in different people, places, and events in your life in ways that are not apparent until you view the entire tapestry of your life (like we have with many of the biblical lives we have studied). That's precisely the problem in this matter of charting God's path for your life. You are viewing the tapestry of your life a few inches at a time. Just as if you were viewing a wall mural from six inches away, you can't see the whole picture. You won't see it until He reveals it to you at the end of your life. So why beat yourself up (and God) because *you* can't figure out the specific path of your life, and *He* won't reveal the details of your life exactly how you think He should? All that does is cause anxiety, anger, or apathy in you. Trust that God has a plan for you and don't obsess about your circumstances (Matthew 6:25-33).

Live in the near term, hope in the long term

Because of the first two ideas, we have to live in the near term. Don't misunderstand that statement. I don't mean something akin to Paul's rebuke in 1 Corinthians 15:32, *"Let us eat and drink for tomorrow we die."* "Live in the near term" doesn't mean "live for today." It isn't some kind of Zen state of mind that says nothing is really good or evil; life is just an experience. Nor is it a "don't worry; be happy" kind of attitude that ignores sorrow and evil in your life. Live in the near term means to take at face value what God gives each day, knowing His plans for our lives are not necessarily completed in a matter of months or years.

God exists outside of physical time and space. Therefore, as we saw in the lives of several people in the Bible, He doesn't seem particularly concerned or hemmed in by time restraints regarding working out the plans He has for our lives. *As His children, neither should we.* That statement implies that we can be content in the near term, knowing that God will complete His plans for us in the long term—however long the "long term" needs to be. It means we can patiently ask questions like, "What lessons does He have for me today?" "What opportunities to help others, to share the Gospel, to learn more about Him will come my way today?" Those are the near term issues He wants us to be focused on. That is part of "...*seek[ing] first His kingdom and His righteousness*..." (Matthew 6:33).

It also means we understand *our near term actions have long term consequences*, both for good and evil. It means that in spite of the seemingly hopeless circumstances we are in, we trust that God will make all things right—whether in this life or the life to come. Our responsibility is to stay in close communion with Him, to understand and obey the known will of God as best we can, and to walk in faith when "detours" arise in the midst of following Him.

My hope and prayer is that you go through your Bible and examine those individuals that resonate more with you based on your present circumstances. As you study their lives and consider the outcome of their actions (both good and bad), I believe God will give you insights into your own disappointments and frustrations with Him. I also believe, if you do this with an open and teachable heart, He will give you victory over those disappointments as well.

ABOUT THE AUTHOR

Ken Hathcoat was involved with the Navigator ministry in college and throughout his twenties. He has developed and taught Christian education curriculum, spoken numerous times from the pulpit and led various small group Bible studies for over thirty years. Ken lives near Fort Collins, Colorado with his wife and two teenage sons.

For more information on When God Disappoints: Character Studies in the Bible, visit our website at: **when-god-disappoints.com**
Or write to me at:
whengoddissapoints@gmail.com

Other Books by Ken Hathcoat

The End: A Study of Revelation and End Time Prophecies

When God Disappoints: Lessons from Jonah

When God Disappoints Pastors